F

You Can Get
Anything
You Want
BUT YOU HAVE TO DO MORE THAN ASK

Roger Dawson

A FIRESIDE BOOK PUBLISHED BY SIMON & SCHUSTER

NEW YORK   LONDON   TORONTO   SYDNEY   TOKYO   SINGAPORE

Copyright © 1985 by Roger Dawson
Illustrations copyright © 1986 by John Caldwell
All rights reserved
including the right of reproduction
in whole or in part in any form
A Fireside Book
Published by Simon & Schuster, Inc.
Simon & Schuster Building
Rockefeller Center
1230 Avenue of the Americas
New York, New York 10020
Originally published by Regency Books
FIRESIDE and colophon are registered trademarks of Simon & Schuster, Inc.
Designed by Christine Swirnoff/Libra Graphics, Inc.
Manufactured in the United States of America
10 9 8 7 6   Pbk.

Library of Congress Cataloging-in-Publication Data

Dawson, Roger.
    You can get anything you want, but you have to do more
than ask.

    "A Fireside book."
    1. Negotiation. I. Title.
[BF637.N4D38 1987]   302.3   86-18436
ISBN 0-671-63439-9 Pbk.

Contents

PREFACE

His listeners gathered around, even the small ones silent with wonder. At 100, the old man's eyes were bright and his mind keen with remembrances of a century, and he could spin a tale of terrifying beauty.

"When I was young, back in the 1980s, things were very, very different," began the ancient voice. "People lived in fear. In many times and many places the streets ran with the blood of young men. Men younger than many of you died for no better reason than to prove that their country was superior to all the others.

"I remember the walls, the iron gates, and the heavy doors that surrounded the houses. Owners bought sophisticated locks and burglar alarms. . . . What was a burglar? Why, a burglar was someone who would sneak into your house and take whatever he needed."

He waited for the oohs and ahs to subside. "Businessmen lived in fear of other businessmen. They fought fiercely to maintain their position in the market, and tried to put each other out of business at every opportunity."

One of his rapt listeners could wait no longer. "But grandpa, how could people live like that?" His young voice quivered with disbelief. "It doesn't make sense to be afraid of other people, especially since we can have anything we want!"

The old man smiled gently and his voice grew distant and thoughtful. "I suppose, in those days, we just didn't know how to negotiate."

INTRODUCTION

At Denver Airport I got in line at the ticket counter behind a large man dressed in greasy blue jeans and a plaid flannel shirt. He was pushing one of those airport shopping carts loaded down with an assortment of sleeping bags, tool kits, and several cardboard boxes sealed with gray strapping tape. "What are you doing," I asked, "moving?"

"Might as well be," he replied. "I'm a truck driver from Philly, and I blew the engine in my truck. I'm going to be out of business for a while, until I can find somebody to lend me the money to fix it, so I'm flying back home. I hope they've got my ticket. My wife took out the last of our savings and sent it to me."

I asked him if he realized that the airline was probably going to charge him a lot of money for his extra pieces of luggage. His suddenly white face told me that he clearly didn't and probably didn't have any way of paying it.

He moved up and I watched him nervously tapping the counter as the clerk searched for his ticket and then started to count his pieces of excess luggage. "Eighty-two dollars excess freight!" the clerk announced with a little too much glee.

My new friend turned to me in despair. "What am I going to do?" he said. "I don't have that kind of money, and I can't leave all of my equipment here!" I asked for permission to do a little negotiating on his behalf, and stepped up to the counter.

A few minutes later the clerk was laughingly tearing up the excess charge slip.

This book is for Harry Johnston, truck driver from Philadelphia, and for anyone else who's been put upon by the big guys and thinks that they can't fight city hall.

It's a book about negotiating, but also a lot more. It's a book about getting everything you want out of life. Everything that you want is owned or controlled by someone else. Isn't it time that we made a study of how to get it?

What this book isn't, is a course on manipulation. It's not a good negotiation unless the other side wins too. I don't know what the best book that's ever been written is—possibly the Bible, or Og Mandino's *Greatest Salesman in the World*, or Napoleon Hill's *Think and Grow Rich*. But I do know what the worst books that have ever been written are—those books on intimidation and power.

There's no need to go through life trying to trick or coerce people out of what you want. If I couldn't get the airline ticket clerk to feel good about tearing up the charge, I was prepared to pay it myself.

A skilled craftsman can turn a block of marble into anything he wants. An unskilled person can turn it into anything except what he wants it to become.

In this book are the skills needed to turn your life into anything you want it to become—but you've got to do more than ask.

CHAPTER 1
The Three Stages of Every Negotiation

If you are not a professional negotiator yet, you may not realize that there are three distinct stages in every negotiation. In fact, as an American you are likely to rush right through stages one and two, eagerly racing for a speedy conclusion in stage three.

Do you golf? Do you remember the first time you approached a tee? You thought the object of the game was to knock the stuffing out of the golf ball, driving it as far and as fast as possible. Contrast that with the form of a professional golfer. Golf is a game of planning and finesse, not a contest to see who can smash a little ball the hardest. The experienced golfer plans his shots. A careful shot onto the fairway, then a shot that will leave the ball on the green, in a good position, and a neat putt from there into the hole.

Do you negotiate? Yes, every day. And yet, chances are you negotiate like the novice golfer plays golf, driving hard and fast for agreement. When Lee Iacocca's negotiating team sits down with the negotiators from the United Auto Workers, you can bet that they go carefully through every stage of a negotiation; the same stages you will learn in this chapter.

I moved to America as an adult, an experience that gave me a unique perspective. As a native American you are probably unaware that you live in a country whose speed control is always set on fast-forward. In the United States rushing is a way of life—it's almost an art. The modern American dream is having what you want, *right now*, without having to go through a lot of nonsense to get it. Learning how to negotiate is very difficult for most Americans and they suffer for their inexperience every time they buy a house, or a car, or even a suit at the clothing store down the block.

You Americans are an impetuous people; your way of life is a never-ending source of amazement and amusement for the rest of the world. In England we have a story about American impetuosity.

It seems there was an elderly British matriarch who always traveled by rail, accompanied by her best friend, a pedigree poodle. She always bought a ticket for her dog so it could have a place to rest its pampered haunches.

One day, while traveling through England in this manner, she was approached by a weary American looking for a seat. The train was full, so the American asked the woman if he might sit down. "Absolutely not," retorted the lady. "Pauline *always* has a seat of her own, and she *always* sits in it!" The desperate man offered to hold the precious pooch in his lap, but to no avail.

Finally the American, in a fit of rage, yanked the window open, grabbed little Pauline by the scruff of her neck, and ejected her into the night air. Slamming the window shut again, he turned and sat in the now vacant seat, to stunned silence in the compartment.

An elderly British gentleman sitting opposite him slowly folded his *Times of London* and took the pipe from his mouth. "That's the trouble with you Americans," he said. "You are so bloody impetuous. Why, you just threw the wrong bitch out the window."

Patience and timing have to be learned. In many countries the learning takes place in every social situation; it is a way of life. Here, you'll have to teach yourself.

I teach negotiating in seminars and workshops across the country, and in some instances it is essential that my students learn the negotiating process. In fact, proper negotiating skills can save lives. When I taught a seminar for 422 California mayors, there was a great deal at stake. So I posed the following situation:

Let's imagine that you are the mayor of a fairly small town and you have just been alerted that there is a sniper in an office building downtown, holding a hostage at gunpoint. Your chief of police has called in reinforcements from the neighboring town, and a S.W.A.T. team will descend like a swarm of deadly wasps in about fifteen minutes, ready to take any action necessary to stop

the sniper, even if it means leveling the whole building.

You rush to the scene, where a megaphone is thrust into your trembling hand. You vaguely recognize your police chief's ashen face. He whispers urgently, "Hurry, we don't have much time. You have to get us out of this mess!" Suddenly, you *have to negotiate*.

This is a tragically common occurrence. Sometimes the man who has his mouth on the megaphone knows how to negotiate; more often, he doesn't. He ran for mayor because he thought he could help the community, or simply because he wanted the prestige. He never planned on anything like this, and more than one life may be lost if he doesn't know how to negotiate.

The Three Stages

The first stage of every negotiation is to find out exactly what the other side wants. *Clarify the objectives.* In the case of the hostage, what does he want? A million dollars? Air time on the local TV? What is he willing to exchange for his demands? Will he free his hostage? The list, of course, is practically endless, and the first stage of every negotiation is to pinpoint what the objectives of the other party are.

The second stage is *gathering information* about the other party; information that may not have anything to do with the demands or needs of that person, but information that will help you tailor your strategy to meet his needs. Who is this person? What motivation compels him to make his demands? Stage two is the preparation stage. Having found out as much as possible about the other person and what his needs are in the negotiation, you are ready to formulate a strategy for stage three.

In the past, stage three is probably the only stage on which you have concentrated your efforts. It is the *agreement* stage where compromises are made and a mutually satisfactory conclusion is reached.

Rushing immediately to stage three rarely leaves both parties satisfied, and when the negotiating process is ignored, the consequences can be tragic.

A few years ago there was a hijacking at the Seattle airport. The plane had been commandeered by a young man who was threatening the crew and passengers with a shoe box full of dynamite. As the plane taxied to the

runway for takeoff, an FBI agent crawled in through the front window. Throwing open the door between the cockpit and the cabin, the agent shot the young man to death. No one knew the young man's name or what he wanted.

After the incident was over, the FBI learned that the hijacker had been an impoverished sixteen-year-old boy with severe physical and mental handicaps. He was unable to speak; the shoe box with which he was threatening his victims was empty. Perhaps most surprising of all was the fact that the boy had pulled the same stunt in the past, and someone had "negotiated" him out of the plane then.

Did the FBI pursue the right course? After all, there was no evidence that the hijacker wasn't serious, and if he was, then the action taken may have saved many lives. But a crisis was resolved with a bullet instead of a negotiation, and a young man is lying today in a grave somewhere instead of getting the help he so desperately needed. What a difference could have been made if the agents had taken the time to go through the stages of negotiation.

Stage one seems to give us the most trouble, doesn't it? Just think of the number of times you have done the following: In stage one you have jumped to conclusions about the other side, without taking the time to find out what the other person really wanted, without giving any chance for explanation.

Jimmy comes to his dad and asks to borrow the car. Immediately his father begins to harangue him: "I am so sick and tired of you borrowing that car all the time. You don't take care of it, you drive like a maniac, and the last time you took it you didn't even bother to put gas in it when you were through." When Dad stops for a breath after fifteen minutes or so of lecturing, Jimmy is finally able to explain that his mother wanted him to go to the store and pick up some medicine for her. Dad could have saved both of them embarrassment and unhappiness by simply taking the time to go through stage one.

Don't jump to conclusions in stage one. Chances are very good that what the other person desperately needs is something not only easily within your ability to deliver, but something it might be in your own best interest to deliver.

For instance, compare the thoughts running through the mind of a potential home buyer and the seller. The buyer is thinking, I just sold my home,

and I'll have to be out in four weeks. If I buy this house I'm going to have to ask the seller to move out almost immediately, and he's not going to like that. The seller is thinking, I just got this terrific job offer in my wife's old hometown and if I don't take it now, she says she'll leave me. I simply have to move within three weeks, and I'm afraid I'll have to drop my price considerably to get a quick sale.

Both the buyer and the seller have the same need, and yet they have both jumped to the conclusion that the other side will be inconvenienced by their demands. If either side takes the time and effort to carefully go through stage one he will discover the other's needs and be able to structure an excellent deal for himself.

Be careful when evaluating the other side as you go through stages one and two. It is an unfortunate fact that it is often necessary to hide the whole truth from the other side in these stages. Be as honest as you feel you need to be, but if you are dealing with an experienced negotiator on the other side of the table, such as Honest Wally of Honest Wally Motors, don't expect total candor.

In countries where negotiating is an art form practiced for the pure joy of bargaining, such tactics are not viewed as being deceitful. The people take a great pride in having hidden needs hiding other hidden needs, and any fool who would enter a negotiation with all of his cards face up deserves the shearing he will receive.

Negotiating is one of the world's oldest games, and if you want to play the game, you have to know the rules. One primary rule is to keep in mind that it is a game. If you want to enjoy the negotiation, accept the need to keep a few of your cards secreted under the table until they are needed. If you, as a buyer, start with your best possible price, you have nowhere to go when it comes time to make compromises.

When you see that dresser at the garage sale, you immediately decide that you will pay not more than thirty dollars. The seller, pointing to the fine Japanese workmanship, claims that this heirloom is worth at least fifty dollars. You, as an honest person, offer thirty dollars. Hard-pressed, the seller backs down to forty-five dollars. Now what? You can raise your offer, paying more than your highest price; you can hold out for thirty dollars, explaining that you have already made your best offer; or you can walk away, cursing that rip-off artist who wanted an arm and a leg for a cheap import.

Negotiating doesn't always involve money; you negotiate every day. Anytime you want something from someone else, and anytime someone wants something from you, you are negotiating. Start now, this minute. Watch for negotiating situations and take the time to go through stages one and two. Find out as much as you can about the other party and find out what their needs are.

You may have already figured out the problem you are going to encounter in many situations, such as when dealing with Honest Wally. You often have little or no control over how much information you are able to gather. Usually the car salesman is not willing to let you have all the information that you would like concerning that particular automobile. In this situation the dealer seems to have all the power. He can tell you what he wants to, not tell you what he doesn't want to, and you — unfortunately — are forced to go directly to stage three.

But wait a minute. Before old Wally ever sets eyes on you, you already know quite a bit about him, don't you? You know what he needs: He needs to sell you a car. In fact, it's customers like you that put food on his table. Who has the power here? Analyzing the limited information you do have gives you the upper hand before you even begin negotiating.

Stage three, finding agreement, is the most crucial stage. If you have done your homework in stages one and two, you can use the techniques that you will learn in this book to your advantage, forging an agreement that satisfies your needs. I will leave further discussion of the entire process of the third stage for other chapters, where we will cover the beginning, middle, and end of that stage separately, and where you will learn tactics that you may choose to use and that will almost certainly be used against you.

Ethics

I have to walk a fine line when trying to balance ethics and good negotiating skills. A good negotiator isn't unethical, in my opinion, when he uses the rules of negotiating to play the game with another experienced player. That is, I wouldn't mind good old Honest Wally using some of the negotiating tactics on me because we would be dealing on the same level. But when he uses those same tactics on John and Mary Smith, who walk onto the lot looking for a good deal, I find his methods extremely unethical.

When you read some the tactics and strategies in the following chapters you are apt to say, "That Roger Dawson! He's the kind of person who would train homing pigeons and then move away."

While standing at the back of the seminar room where I am about to teach, I have overheard people sitting in front of me — unaware that I was there, of course — saying things like: "Just wait until you hear this guy. He's the kind of guy who could get the gold right out of your teeth."

In my defense, I can only say that the tactics discussed are an inherent part of negotiating. You may think: I'm much too honest to ever use strategies like *that*. I don't feel comfortable doing that sort of thing. And that's fine. But even if you never once use the tactics I'm going to discuss, you need to understand the dynamics of them and the reasoning behind them, as well as how to fight back. Because, believe me, whether you use them or not, they are being used against you all the time.

As you read and learn more about negotiating, I want you to start thinking about how many times a day you negotiate. Start to use the techniques in this book every time you are asked for something. You will be surprised at how quickly they'll take effect, and the agreements that you make every day will be reached more easily, and probably more in your favor. Try it!

SUCCESS COMMENTARY

Do What You Fear

If I had to choose one single exercise that would most improve the quality of a person's life, it would be this: Do what you fear. Your fears are all like monkeys on your back, weighing you down and preventing you from enjoying your life to the fullest.

What do you fear? Or what do you avoid for no better reason than the fact that you feel uncomfortable doing it. (Admit it: the real reason you avoid it is that you are afraid.)

A common fear is one that the medical establishment will one day recognize and name *telephobia*; the fear of telephones. How would you feel as a Red Cross volunteer assigned to call every telephone number listed in three pages of your phone book? How successful would you be as a telephone salesman calling people every evening and trying to sell them sets of World Book encyclopedias? Do you want to conquer that fear, so that you can pick up a phone with impunity and feel completely at ease talking to anyone (except maybe those infernal answering machines, which *nobody* feels comfortable talking to)?

The answer is to do what you fear. Are you near a phone right now? Pick it up and dial a local number at random. When the other party answers, speak right up: "Hello, this is Joe from World Book, and I'm calling to talk to you about purchasing a set of our encyclopedias." Let them hang up on you, and then pick up the phone and dial another number and do the same thing again. Once you have called five or six people (people who were probably enjoying their favorite show or a nice, hot bath) you will have conquered that fear. Don't call more than about six, though; on about the seventh call the joker at the other end is liable to say, "Hey, I might be interested in that. How much are they?" And then what do you say?

Go ahead, do it now. I'll wait right here.

Did you do it? If your heart froze and you couldn't force yourself to do it, then you are still carrying that monkey. Worse, you just fed that fear by allowing it to conquer you. Come on, try again. Don't let any fear run your life.

Everyone has their own unique set of fears, I thought, as I dropped through the sky like a rock. My greatest fear—a monkey slightly larger than King Kong—had been the fear of jumping out of an airplane. The thought of facing the earth so far away with only a parachute to save me from falling at a velocity that threatened to tear my heart—a heart I had grown quite fond of, by the way—right out of my body?

I had no reason to believe that I would ever have to jump from a plane, but I wanted to overcome all of my fears and had decided that taking on the biggest one (short of death) would be a good place to start.

So it was not actually a death wish that propelled me out to the Perris Airport to attend a one-day course in the fine art of watching your own body plummet earthward from 3,000 feet. As the classwork progressed, I made a remarkable observation: Fear is reduced in direct proportion to knowledge. As my knowledge of parachute jumping increased, my fear of jumping decreased, until by the time they trundled us onto the plane, my fear had subsided to the size of an adult gorilla. A very mean adult gorilla.

As I stood at the door of the plane watching the earth pass so far below, I realized that I had reached the moment of truth. Would I continue to let this fear rule me or would I be able to free myself of this burden once and for all?

I had to decide whether or not to take my instructor—who was five feet six and claimed to have been six feet three when he took the job—seriously. Perhaps he had noticed my glazed eyes, or the way my body shook uncontrollably. Maybe it was the way I stammered and drooled. I don't know, but he decided I was the one to pick on. As we were approaching the jump site he said, "Now Roger, as you fall I want you to put your right hand behind your head with your elbow extended, and your left hand behind your back, also with your elbow extended."

I didn't remember any such instruction in class, so I asked, "What is the purpose of that?"

"Well," he said with a broad grin, "if your chute fails to open, it makes it so much easier for us to unscrew you out of the ground."

The guy was full of laughs. It didn't help at all when, as I stood trembling at the door of the plane and my instructor prepared to throw me out bodily, I asked him how long it would take to hit the ground if my chute didn't open. "The rest of your life," he said, and out I went.

I must have survived the fall because I am sitting here now, writing this book. Although I was petrified most of the way down, I must admit the experience was exhilarating. By the time I reached the ground again, I had managed to remove that monkey. Well, maybe not entirely, but it was no bigger than an infant spider monkey.

Do the thing that scares you. What the fear is doesn't matter; public, private, large or small—just do it. (Unless you happen to fear bank robbing.)

When you are making a list of things you need to do, why not do the one you fear most first? As my friend Danny Cox says, "If you have some frogs to swallow, my suggestion is that you swallow the biggest, ugliest frog first, and do it first thing in the morning." In other words, get those things out of the way early and the rest of your day won't have to be filled with dread.

Do what scares you—and then nothing will!

CHAPTER 2
Beginning
Gambits

Understanding the stages of a negotiation is essential if you want to play the negotiating game; knowing those stages is a rule every player needs to play well. When you face an opponent across a chessboard, there is no sense in playing a game if either player doesn't understand how the pieces move.

You know how the pieces in a negotiation move now, but that isn't enough—you need strategy. In chess, any maneuver for advantage is called a *gambit*. It is a preplanned strategy intended to give the player an advantage in the game, even it if means sacrificing a pawn for a better position. There are beginning gambits, to get the game moving in the direction you want it to go; there are middle gambits to keep the game going your way; and there are ending gambits to guide your opponent into checkmate. When you face an opponent in a negotiation, whether the issue is who will do the dishes or bilateral nuclear disarmament, you will need gambits—moves for advantage.

In this chapter we will look at some beginning gambits; tactics that you will use at the opening (or even before the actual opening) of a negotiation.

The Role of Reluctance

Most beginning gambits are game plans laid out by both parties before stage three of the negotiation—seeking agreement—ever occurs. They deal primarily with the attitude you are presenting to the person with whom you are negotiating.

The first attitude is that of the reluctant buyer or reluctant seller. *Always* be reluctant. Remember, you are not being forced to buy or sell, and in some cases you may not feel very compelled to buy or sell at all and you want the other negotiator to know that.

It should be fairly obvious that if you approach a seller bubbling over with enthusiasm for his product, you are going to be faced with an uphill battle for price concessions. And yet this first, basic rule is violated everywhere. If you want to watch this in action, take a little time and observe the buyers on a car lot. (You will notice that I use a car lot example quite a bit, but it is undoubtedly the best example of an uneven negotiating match. Car salespeople are highly trained in negotiating tactics.)

Just watch as Clyde Kadiddlehopper runs his hand admiringly over the satin finish on that VW bug. He *wants* that car. Now watch as Honest Wally approaches; if his smile got any broader it would literally be touching his ears. "Now there's a *car*, my friend, and you look like the kind of guy who needs a good car. Howdy, I'm Honest Wally"– and his hand appears, as if from nowhere, practically dripping with sincere friendship. Clyde admits that his last car just broke down and that he has always wanted a bug just like this one. Wally obviously wants to help out, and he is so understanding of Clyde's problem that he's practically willing to give the little bug away.

What chance does Clyde have in a negotiation like this? If you were a knight in a jousting tournament, how would you feel if you had no shield? Don't go into a negotiation without the shield of reluctance.

I used to know an extremely rich and powerful investor, a man who owned real estate all over town. He probably owned fifty million dollars worth of real estate, owed about thirty-five million in loans, and therefore had a net worth of about fifteen million dollars. Very successful; what you would call a heavy hitter. He liked wheeling and dealing.

Like many investors, his strategy was simple: buy a property, hold onto it and let it appreciate, then sell at a higher price. Many smaller investors would bring him purchase offers for one of his holdings, eager to acquire one of his better-known properties. But this well-seasoned investor knew how to use the gambit of the reluctant seller.

He would read an offer quietly, and when he was finished he would

25

slide it thoughtfully back across the table, scratch above one ear, and say something like, "I don't know. Of all my properties, I have very special feelings for this one. I was thinking of keeping it and giving it to my daughter for a college graduation present, and I really don't think that I would be interested in parting with it for anything less than the full asking price. You understand; this particular property is worth a great deal to me. But look; it was nice of you to bring in an offer for me, and in all fairness, so that you won't have wasted all your time, what is the very best price that you feel you could give me?"

The professional reluctant seller always tries to edge up the buyer's negotiating range before the real negotiating ever begins.

Planning

The most important phase of any negotiation is the period of time after you realize you will be negotiating and before the actual confrontation begins. You will have to lay your plans based on the personality of your opponent, your own negotiating range, how reluctant you will be, and a hundred other things. In short, every gambit should be planned in advance.

The first thing to determine is your negotiating range. Just how little or how much are you willing to give up to achieve your objectives? Your range is your clear, well thought out (preferably written) idea of the price you want. Your negotiating range should not only include the best price you could possibly hope for, and the price that you expect you'll probably get after all the negotiating, but also the very lowest price you could possibly settle on. If you have planned your range well, and if you stick to it, you may reasonably expect the final agreement to fall somewhere in that range.

Even without a written range, everyone always has a mental negotiating range. For instance, a seller may be thinking, I've advertised this property for $60,000 and I wish I could find somebody to take it off my hands for that much. But I'd be willing to take $55,000 just to get that land off my mind. I only hope I don't have to go as low as $50,000 to get rid of it, but if I don't get any offers I might have to dump it that low. This seller's negotiating range is from $50,000 to $60,000.

PRACTICE "THE FLINCH" BEFORE EVERY MAJOR PURCHASE...

The buyer's range could be much lower than that, say, from $35,000 to $45,000. The really serious negotiating range, then, is from $45,000 to $50,000, and that is the range that will give the negotiators the most problems. It is here that reluctance can make or break a deal.

A reluctant buyer (or an eager buyer playing a reluctant role) would say to the seller, "I'm really not very interested—this isn't quite what I had in mind—but just to be fair to you, what is the very lowest price that you would accept for this property?"

The prudent seller responds by not bringing his price down all the way to the low end of his range, but he could very well say, "I guess for a quick sale I might be willing to sell for as little as, oh, $55,000." There remains a difference of $10,000 between the buyer's range and the seller's range, but the difference has dropped from a spread of the advertised price of $60,000 to the buyer's desired high of $45,000. And that's definitely a much better place from which to start negotiating.

Bear in mind that the final, agreed-upon price will frequently be near the midpoint between the seller's and the buyer's opening bids. That is the point that seems the most fair and logical in every negotiation. You say twenty and I say ten. Where will we end up? Probably at fifteen. It's no different when I say $20,000 or even $200,000. We will end up close to the middle. So determine your negotiating range before you begin bidding, and always leave room for compromise.

The Flinch

The next tactic is flinching, and there is no tactic as easy to use or as effective as a good flinch. Get into the habit of reacting visibly whenever you hear the price of something. Obvious shock, disgust, or disbelief can accomplish incredible things.

For example, imagine Bill, the average tourist, walking along the sidewalk at a resort area, the Nikon around his neck riding comfortably on his Hawaiian print shirt. He stops for a minute to admire the charcoal-sketch artist and out of curiosity asks how much a sketch will cost. The artist, flicking a wrist at the easel, says, "Fifteen dollars." No visible reaction on the part of Bill, so the artist casually adds, "and five dollars for color." He watches his victim carefully. Still no reaction. "And with our special wrapping and packaging it'll come to thirty dollars." That seems a little much to our friend Bill, but he thinks, What the heck, these tourist places always cost more, and this may be my only trip to California.

Five minutes after Bill has walked away with his prize, Robin approaches the artist.

"How much for a portrait?"

"Fifteen dollars."

Robin, who understands the power of a good flinch, claps her hand to her cheek in consternation. "Fifteen dollars! That's a lot of money for one charcoal sketch!"

The artist wants to make a sale, so he quickly adds, "Look, I'll tell you what. I normally charge an extra five dollars if you want color, but for you I'll throw it in at no extra charge."

But Robin is on a roll. Mouth open wide with astonishment, she says, "I assumed your price included color. You mean you usually charge fifteen dollars for a black and white sketch?"

The artist looks like a kid caught with his hand in the cookie jar. "Okay, okay. Fifteen dollars for a color portrait, and I'll throw in this special wrapping and packaging too. Good enough?"

Somewhat mollified, Robin sits for her portrait.

The power of the flinch will not be underestimated or overlooked by the experienced negotiator. I've taught this technique many, many times, and my students have always been amazed at what they can accomplish with this simple tactic.

In Boston, at one of the plushest restaurants in one of the plushest hotels in the city, a student of one of my seminars was able to get the price on a bottle of fine wine reduced simply because she tried this gambit. A man who had taken the same course was able to get two thousand dollars off the price of a Corvette when he tried it.

A close friend of mine, who conducts seminars, too, decided to try the same tactic in a negotiation. He went to a company in southern California and proposed that they hire him to put on seminars for them. When he had finished his presentation, the company's spokesman said, "We might be interested in having you work for us, but we should tell you that the highest offer we can give you is fifteen hundred dollars."

As it happened, that was exactly the fee my friend was charging at the time, and he was about to accept, when he decided to try the flinch. "Fifteen hundred dollars!" he exclaimed in hurt tones. "I can't afford to do it for just fifteen hundred dollars."

The spokesman frowned thoughtfully. "Well," he said, "the most we've ever offered any speaker is twenty-five-hundred dollars, but that is the very best we can do." That was one thousand dollars in about twenty seconds. Not bad for one flinch.

"But I'm not like that. I could never be so theatrical. I would be mortified at the thought of pulling a stunt like that." That's the way my wife is.

In a store she'll walk up to the salesperson and ask, "How much is that coat?" Following her gaze to the luxurious mink, the clerk's eyes light up.

"That one is only two thousand dollars, ma'am."

My wife thinks for a moment, smiles, and while I collapse onto the floor in the background, she says, "That's not bad!"

I have a wonderful wife, but she thinks flinching is dumb and ridiculous and melodramatic. I think it would have been interesting to see how much that mink would have cost after a bit of judicious astonishment. It's worth overcoming your embarrassment at reacting.

Negotiating is a game, remember? One of the rules of the game says that flinching is okay, and that the winners know how to use this gambit effectively. Swallow that false pride and play the game. It's fun.

Feel/Felt/Found Theory

Never argue up front. This is a basic public relations principle. Whatever the person you're negotiating with says to you as he begins his proposal, do not argue with it. Agree with him instead. Whenever you argue an issue, the other negotiator feels honor bound to defend his point and prove himself right.

At my seminars I usually ask someone in the front row to stand. As I hold my two hands together, with my palms facing toward the person I've asked to stand, I ask her to place her hand against mine. Having done that, and without saying another word, I start to push against the other person. Automatically, without any instruction, she begins to push back. People shove when they are shoved.

Verbal pushing happens all the time. If you represent the ABC company and your opponent represents XYZ, you will find yourselves placed in adversarial positions. He says the weather is fine and you remark that it could be a little cooler for your comfort. Pretty soon, before you even get into the main topic of negotiation, he is insisting that the earth is round and you are equally adamant that it is flat.

Don't start a negotiation by arguing, no matter how much you might disagree. Use the feel/felt/found tactic. It is a time-honored approach used by every professional negotiator, every day. Take someone who says to me, "Roger, that is without a doubt the most outrageous and objectionable proposal that I have ever heard in my entire life. I don't have any idea where you got the unmitigated gall to say something like that to me." (Women say that to me all the time.) I answer, calmly, "I understand the way you feel. Many other people have felt exactly the same way. However, I have found that if we sit down and reason this thing out together, it's much easier to reach an agreement."

Feel/felt/found is a very easy method of addressing conflict. You can answer any controversial issue or argumentative statement by explaining that you understand how the other person *feels*. In fact, you mention, he is not alone. Many other people have *felt* exactly the same way about that same issue. Finally you explain that you have studied the problem and have *found* a solution.

An example of this technique might be the dealer in the sales department of a foreign car dealership. The salesperson makes his proposal to the prospective buyer, who responds with, "No, I know all about foreign cars. They always have problems, and when they break down the spare parts are either unavailable or they cost a fortune. Thanks anyway, but I am not going to get roped into buying an import."

Of course, the seller could answer, "Look, mister, I don't know where you got that crazy idea, because you're completely wrong about these cars. We don't have half the problems those domestic car companies have, and your ideas are way out of line." With a sales pitch like that the salesman wouldn't be able to sell hay to a horse.

A good salesman will answer, "You know, I understand exactly how you feel. You might be surprised to learn that a lot of other people that I've talked to have felt exactly the same way—people who are now driving our cars. I say that because after we started looking into the reasons for the feelings that you yourself have expressed, and examined in detail this particular make and year of car, we found that there are 172 distributors in the nation. There are 284 service depots, and in the last year of requests for parts, the average delivery time for a part not in stock was only 26.32 hours. So really, there is no foundation at all for that feeling. Quite frankly, I suspect that it was a rumor started in Detroit."

A buyer in that situation would be much more inclined to listen and maybe even change his position.

The feel/felt/found theory is a basic element of diplomacy; agree with people until they agree with you. Establish rapport at the beginning of every negotiation and your opponent won't feel like your enemy.

Sir Winston Churchill, a fellow countryman, was an expert at this sort of thing. He was a grand old man and he loved to drink, socialize, and entertain. One night Lady Astor, who at the time happened to be in favor of prohibition in England, approached Winston and said, "Mr. Churchill, you are disgusting. And you are drunk!"

Winston Churchill did not argue with her point of view. Rather, he agreed with Lady Astor: "You are absolutely right. I *am* drunk. But *you* are ugly, and in the morning, *I* shall be sober."

Churchill found himself in many situations where his caustic wit turned the tables in an argument. There was the famous argument between him and Lady Astor when she exclaimed in rage, "Winston, if I were married to you, I should poison your tea!"

He looked up with marvelous self-control and said, "Lady Astor, if I were married to you, I should drink it."

There was also the incident when he had been invited by Lady Astor to her country estate for dinner. They were being served chicken and she asked, "Winston, what would you like?"

Churchill answered, "I think I'd like a piece of that breast."

Lady Astor was somewhat appalled, and with great dignity she reprimanded her guest: "Winston, that's rather crude, don't you agree? In this house, at my table, we always refer to our choice as either white meat or dark meat."

"Winston Churchill lived by the rule that one should not argue, at least not openly."

The next day Churchill sent Lady Astor a lovely corsage with a note attached that read simply, "Lady Astor, you would do me a great honor if you would pin this to your white meat."

Winston Churchill was a true diplomat. He lived by the rule that one should not argue, at least not openly. He was always able to make his point, but he did so without creating an argumentative atmosphere, and he generally had the last word.

The feel/felt/found tactic should always be employed when faced with an adversary bent on disagreement. Go out of your way to placate the other person in every negotiation; not only will the effort pay off many times over, but the person is much more likely to return to your negotiating table again and again.

The "Want It All" Approach

There was once a very old couple who lived in a small, somewhat sordid thatched hut in a tiny village. One day, a particularly nasty storm blew through the village, completely demolishing the hut. Being much too old and poor to rebuild, the couple moved in with their daughter and her husband. This arrangement, of course, precipitated a rather unpleasant domestic situation, as the daughter's hut was barely big enough for herself, her husband, and their four small children.

The poor woman of the house went to the wise man of the village, told him the problem, and asked, "Whatever shall we do?"

The wise man puffed quietly on his pipe for a minute before responding. "You have chickens, don't you?"

"Yes," she answered. "We have ten chickens."

"Then bring the chickens into your home with you."

As a solution his suggestion seemed ludicrous to the woman, but she obeyed. The problem was soon unbearable, with feathers as well as words now flying about the hut. The woman returned to the wise man, pleading once again for advice.

"You have pigs, do you not?"

"Yes, we have three pigs."

"Then you must bring the pigs into your home with you."

That seemed positively ridiculous but to disobey the wise man was unthinkable, so she brought the pigs into the hut. And now life was truly unlivable, with eight people, ten chickens, and three pigs sharing one tiny, noisy hut.

The next day the woman, fearing for her sanity, approached the wise man for the last time. "Please," she cried, "we cannot live like this. Tell me what to do and we'll do it, but please, help us."

This time the wise man's response was encouraging: "Remove the chickens and the pigs from your home."

The animals were quickly evicted and the entire family lived together happily for the rest of their days.

For negotiators this fable illustrates the value of the "want it all" gambit. By acting as though you are demanding the world, the sun, and the moon when you begin the negotiation, you will find that you can often get the other side to give you the world if you will throw out the sun and the moon. When you make an offer you should act as though this is the only chance you will have to present your demands, one chance and one only to ask for everything you want.

The reasoning behind this strategy is twofold. The first justification for making such outrageous demands is that you might just get what you ask for. What you think is an outrageous demand will sometimes be well within your opponent's negotiating range. The second reason is that by asking for more than you really want, you are creating a climate conducive to compromise. You are giving yourself enough leeway so you can lose one or two points of the argument—and that means, of course, that the other side can win one or two points of the argument—and still come out with a good deal.

A friend of mine who works with real estate in Texas was helping a buyer in the purchase of a piece of land. They had a fairly satisfactory contract but then they started thinking of other things they would like to ask for, and they came up with a list of twenty-three paragraphs of demands they wanted to present to the seller. Naturally, they felt sure that at least half of these new demands would be rejected, but they could be satisfied that they would probably get at least some of the things they were asking for.

To their amazement the seller came back to the negotiating table and argued vehemently against one sentence in the eighteenth paragraph. And my friend, the negotiator, didn't give in easily. They quibbled about that one sentence for quite some time, until finally, reluctantly, my friend conceded the paragraph to the seller. The seller then got up and left the negotiating table, feeling that he had won a sizable victory—despite the fact that he had conceded the remaining twenty-two paragraphs of demands. In that case the negotiator who used the one-and-only tactic got everything and more.

That example also illustrates the most important part of this gambit. When the seller left the table he did so feeling like a winner. This is the underlying theory in win-win negotiating.

When you prepare your opening demands, ask for the other party to take in the chickens, the pigs, and maybe even a horse or two. They will be so thrilled to have the pigs and the horses thrown out that they will be happy living with the chickens.

If you have ever taken a two- or three-year old shopping, you know that they seem to have a natural ability to use this gambit on you. They want Pac-Man cereal, and they want those little colored marshmallows, and they want Pop-Tarts, and they want . . . everything. Your youngster leaves the store chomping on a piece of gum, and you think you won.

Don't ever be afraid to ask for more than you expect to settle for. Not only is it a good negotiating strategy for getting more, but it also leaves room for fair play and good feelings.

First Offers

Never jump at the first offer, no matter how good it looks. There is a story which, while somewhat apocryphal, is an excellent example of what can happen when you jump at an offer.

There was a very famous movie star, a woman who had just made it big and was looking for a house suited to her new position. She finally found exactly what she had been looking for, but unfortunately, the advertised price was much higher than what her new but still very unsteady budget would allow. This was some time ago and the house was priced at a then quite expensive $250,000.

She decided to approach the broker anyway, just to see what his response would be to what she felt was a ridiculously low offer. She felt that if the broker would at least negotiate with her, she would feel encouraged, possibly even tempted to buy the house. Her proposition to the broker was simple: "I'm somewhat interested in the house you have listed in Beverly Hills for $250,000. I can offer $175,000 for it."

The broker's answer was equally simple and to the point. "We'll take it," he said.

So the movie star got a fantastic buy on a house that has doubled and tripled in value since then. And yet, whenever she speaks of her house and how she got it, she always concludes with the statement, "I have to be the world's worst negotiator."

That's quite a statement, coming from someone who made such a terrific bargain. But the important question is, Why doesn't she end with the statement, "I have to be the world's best negotiator?" The answer is because the broker jumped at her first offer. It's really an error of social grace, rather than strictly a negotiating tactic.

What if, instead of his blundering acceptance, the broker had said, "I'm terribly sorry, but $175,000 will not be regarded as a serious offer by me or by my clients. I do, however, have a fiduciary obligation to present all offers to them for consideration. If you'll excuse me for a moment, I'll go next door and call in the offer, as a courtesy to you." And returning a minute later, he would have said, "I just cannot believe it, but this must be your lucky day! Of course, they rejected the offer of $175,000, but they came down much lower than I ever expected them to, and they said they'll accept an offer of $185,000." The movie star would gladly have paid the extra $10,000 to be able to say that she was "the world's best negotiator."

What would your own reaction be if you were to propose a ridiculously low offer and it was immediately accepted? For example, suppose you see a car you particularly like advertised for $10,000. Your opening offer is what you consider to be an extremely low proposal of $6,000, and as you expect to split the difference, you think that you will probably end up paying around $8,000.

With nerves of steel and all the courage you can muster you announce your offer, bracing yourself for the roar of laughter that you expect to come from the salesman when you are finished. Instead, he says, "Okay,

we'll take it." How do you feel?

You probably have two reactions. The first is by far the more dangerous to the safe completion of the negotiation. It is the thought, What's wrong with the car that they're willing to get rid of it at such a low price? What's wrong here that I didn't figure out? The negotiations may grind to a halt because of the too-quick acceptance of a first offer.

The second reaction is monetary. I could have done better, you think. And you would probably think that even if you'd proposed $2,000 instead of $6,000. No matter how low the price they accept is, if they accept it too quickly, you will always feel as if you could have done better and that in some subtle way you've been cheated.

Actually, you have been cheated; you have been cheated out of the chance to negotiate. I had a personal experience with this principle several years ago, when I was president of a real estate company in southern California. It was a large company with twenty-eight offices and more than 500 sales associates.

One day a magazine salesman came in to see me, trying to sell me advertising space in his magazine. I was familiar with the magazine and it was an excellent opportunity, and I very much wanted our company to be a part of it. He gave me an offer I could have quickly accepted, for it was very reasonable: $2,000.

I love to negotiate, and I couldn't pass up the opportunity. So I began to use some of these gambits with him. Eventually I got his price down to only $800. By then I couldn't help but feel, My goodness, if he came down from $2,000 to $800 that quickly, I wonder just how low I can get him to go. So I used a middle gambit called "higher authority," and I said to him, "This looks fine, but I do have to run it by my board of directors before the deal can be closed. Luckily, they are meeting this evening. I'll take it to them tonight and I'll get back to you in a couple of days with a final okay."

Because I was really curious as to how well I could do, I called the salesman back a few days later and said: "You will never know how embarrassed I am about this. You know, I really felt that I wouldn't have any problem at all selling the board of directors on that $800 offer you quoted me, but they are so difficult to deal with right now—the budget's been giving everyone headaches lately. Anyway, to make a long story short, they did come back with a counter offer, but it's so low I don't know if I can even tell you what it is without laughing myself."

The salesman, of course, wanted to hear the board's counter offer, so I said, "They say they won't go a penny over $500."

I nearly dropped the phone when he answered, "That's okay, I'll take it." And I felt cheated. I had made him lower his price from $2,000 to $500, and I still felt that I could have done better. I felt cheated because he had taken my low offer too quickly; I was negotiating with him, but he was not negotiating with me. We both walked away from that negotiation feeling like losers.

Some years after this incident I had the chance to meet the salesman again, this time immediately after one of my lectures, in which he had listened to me tell that story. After the seminar he approached from the back of the room. I have to admit I wondered what he would think after hearing what I'd done to him.

But he came up to me, shook my hand, and said with a smile: "I can't thank you enough for explaining that to me. I had no idea the impact that my tendency to jump at a quick deal was having on people. I'll never do that again!"

Turning down the first offer you receive may be very difficult. Perhaps you have been trying to sell your home for six months and you finally get a decent offer. You will be tempted to grab it quickly. But if you do, the person making the offer may begin to wonder why, and that is a risky question to be asking in the middle of a transaction.

Remember the advantages of waiting awhile and negotiating. It can be quite beneficial—to the pocketbook as well as the ego.

Agreeable Means Able to Agree

The manner in which you make your initial proposal is extremely important. You should always ask for much more than you expect to get, but you must imply a certain amount of flexibility in your demands. Both in proposing and in rejecting proposals, leave a little leeway—a little slack in the line—that will let the other person know you are willing to negotiate.

Making a "take it or leave it" offer puts the other person in a defensive position, and if your offer does not fit in their negotiating range it will probably be left rather than taken. The take it or leave it approach won't even get to the table, while an agreeable attitude leads to working out the solution to the disagreement.

This principle of agreeability leads to an interesting corollary. Say you want to buy the $10,000 car for $7,000. It is always much better to enter the negotiating process with an offer of $6,000 and the promise of flexibility than to propose your offer of $7,000 and no flexibility. If you begin with your best offer, and don't hold out the chance that you might be willing to give a little in the dealings, there is no way that a climate can be created in which the other party can feel good about the deal; there's no way he can feel he has gained something from the transaction.

On the other hand, if you enter the bargaining with your offer of $6,000 and flexibility, even though you know your offer will be rejected, the negotiations will be much more fruitful and a great deal easier. When you finally settle on your desired price of $7,000, you have won because you are getting the price you wanted, and the seller has won because he is getting $1,000 more than you were initially offering.

The Vise

The last of the beginning gambits is the vise. Not a medieval device for torturing a price concession, the vise is an innocuous-sounding sentence that has a remarkable effect on the other negotiator; seven words that will put any person on the spot; seven words that are probably more effective than any medieval device could hope to be: "You'll have to do better than that."

There is only one good response to that question, and it is imperative that you know both the question and the response. Like many opening gambits in chess it is so well known by experienced players that it's rarely used in professional circles. But it is likely to be used often on you, and you should be prepared.

A good negotiator responds to the vise with: "And just how much better do I have to do?" putting the pressure back on the vise user. However, an inexperienced negotiator will often give away a rather large chunk of his negotiating range just because his opponent used that simple phrase.

When the prospective buyer asks the salesman for the price of that car, the salesman answers, "ten thousand dollars." The prospective buyer sadly shakes his head and says simply, "You'll have to do better than that." The salesman is immediately under pressure to do "better than that." He may say, "Well, for a quick sale I guess I could let it go for $9,500." You may not be willing to pay $9,500 either, but it's still a much better place to begin your negotiating from. With seven words you have squeezed his negotiating range by $500.

A good example of the power of the vise is a story that is sometimes told about Henry Kissinger. The incident took place while he was Secretary of State under President Nixon, during the Vietnam War.

Early in the conflict he had an undersecretary of State prepare a very extensive paper for him on the conflict in Vietnam. It was extremely comprehensive; leather-bound, gold-engraved. Very impressive, thought the undersecretary as he sent the report to Kissinger for approval. Several days later, however, the document was returned with a note attached reading: "You will have to do better than this. H.K."

The undersecretary worked over every page of the report, adding reports and copies of reports detailing every aspect of the situation. Satisfied that he had completed a true work of bureaucratic art, he submitted it once again, only to find it returned with the same note attached.

Chagrined, the undersecretary redoubled his efforts, working over the document until he was sure it was beyond reproach. He added pictures, charts, and graphs, and the document became thicker and thicker, until it was quite a monumental volume. The undersecretary was apprehensive, so he delivered the report to Kissinger personally.

"Mr. Kissinger," he said, "please don't send this back to me again. I've worked so hard on this. It's just not going to get any better; this is the best I can do."

Mr. Kissinger took the leather-bound volume and placed it squarely in front of him. "In that case, I guess I'll read it."

Teachers, pressed for time and with a hundred reports stacked on their desks, will return papers to their students with a vise attached: "You'll have to do better than this." And they know that the papers will come back better than they were the first time. There is *always* room for improvement from the other side, and the vise will squeeze the other person's negotiating range.

Of course, all of these gambits—beginning, middle, and ending—are strategies, and the use of strategies implies very careful planning. In the following chapters you will notice that every gambit, every advance in the negotiations, will be dependent on the atmosphere that has been created in the first stage of the transaction. The demands you make and the attitude you present should be determined by a carefully laid plan that encompasses the entirety of the negotiation. Your opening gambits, based on a careful evaluation of your opponent, will win or lose the game for you.

You have planned and executed your opening gambits. The handshakes and opening offers have been completed, and it's time for the *real* dealing to begin.

SUCCESS COMMENTARY

The Rules of Life

When my youngest son was thirteen, he bought a Christmas present for me. It was a game called Othello. This game is played with a board similar to a chessboard, with a large number of buttons that are black on one side and white on the other. The object is to fill the board with your color markers. As you and your opponent take turns, each putting one piece down at a time, anytime one of your markers is caught between two of your opponent's markers it is flipped over and becomes his marker. When the board is filled, the player with the most markers wins.

Nothing to it, right? We played a game and I was somewhat surprised at my son's luck. After ten games in which I was soundly defeated I began to suspect that more than luck was involved. Using a negotiating tactic ("I won't play with you anymore"), I gently coerced him into revealing his strategy.

It turns out that there are three basic principles in Othello which, when applied religiously, no matter how illogical they seem at the time, will virtually guarantee a winning game against a player who is not using the same principles.

Wouldn't it be something if there were three basic principles that would guarantee success in life? Three simple strategies that we could consistently apply to get everything we wanted—imagine it for a moment.

I'll give you three such principles. Right now. But you have to promise to apply them—I hate wasting such valuable information. I have studied the lives of many successful people, and in every case they have used three simple rules for living. None of them are secrets; anybody can use them. Including you.

First and foremost, I believe in the principle of goal setting. The people who have had great success in life use goals to guide them. Goal setting has been cited as the cause for the success of people such as Werner von Braun, who built a rocket and sent it to the moon, and Ray Kroc, who took a little hamburger stand in San Bernardino, California, and turned it into a worldwide enterprise—McDonald's.

They knew exactly where they wanted to go, and they implanted that goal deeply into the fabric of their lives. They worked hard to achieve their goals, and they eventually found themselves right where they wanted to be.

The second principle of success is time management. No successful person can afford to squander time aimlessly. Those goals won't be accomplished by coming home at the end of a workday, collapsing into your overstuffed chair and flicking on the TV. Daily planning is absolutely essential for reaching your goals, and following those plans will guarantee your success.

Third is a strong sense of positive expectancy. On a very windy day I watched several people making their way carefully down a street, fighting the strong gusts even though they were moving in the same direction as the wind. Then I saw two boys, about ten years old, on skateboards, holding a garbage-can lid in each hand, arms extended and whipping down the same sidewalk. They screamed past the laboring pedestians, laughing and enjoying the wind's gale force.

Without a positive attitude you may set goals and move toward them with determination, but you will do so fighting all the way. Even though you are headed in the right direction, you will constantly resist any positive influences that would otherwise push you right along. A person with an attitude filled with positive expectations lives in a world filled with exciting possibilities.

The three strategies for winning in Othello aren't secrets, and yet my son was able to win every game simply by applying those strategies consistently. It is no different with the principles of goal setting, time management, and positive expectations. If you want to win this game called life, apply those strategies consistently.

CHAPTER 3
Middle Gambits

Now the game is under way. You have established the other person's objectives and negotiating range. You have made your want-it-all offer and, hopefully, squeezed his negotiating range with a carefully applied vise. It's time to get down to brass tacks and try to establish a basis for agreement. You now need some middle gambits to keep the game moving in the right direction.

A Higher Authority

At first glance it would seem that any negotiation would go better when the negotiators themselves have the authority to make final decisions. If each party could say to the other, "I know what I am doing and I have the power to get the best deal possible," it seems as though the bargaining process would be much easier. Strangely enough, this is not the case. In fact, any negotiator who enters a discussion as the obvious authority from his side has put himself at a severe bargaining disadvantage.

The reason is simple. When you have the authority to make the final decision, your opponent knows that he only has to convince you. He doesn't have to work quite as hard to give you the benefits of a deal if you are the final authority. Once you have given your okay, the deal is consummated.

Not so with the person who has to answer to a higher authority. When you have to have approval from your board of directors, or the stockholders, or your partner, or even your spouse, then the other negotiator must do much more than convince you; he must present a deal that you can take to your higher authority for approval. He knows that he must completely win you over to his side so you will *want* to convince your board of directors that this is a good deal.

Keep in mind that a shrewd negotiator will use the same gambit on you, given the chance. If you want to see this gambit used, visit any car dealer in town and sit down to talk price with him. After some preliminary negotiating, you may be surprised to find your low offer almost immediately accepted. After getting you to commit yourself to a price (which sets you up psychologically to accept the idea that you *will* buy that car), the salesman will say something like, "Well, this looks good. All I have to do is run this by my manager for his approval and the car is yours."

You can feel the car keys and pink slip in your hand already, and you are sitting there congratulating yourself on getting such a good deal, when he returns with the sales manager. The manager sits down and reviews the price with you. He says, "You know, Fred was a little out of line here." Fred looks properly embarrassed. "This price is almost $500 under our factory invoice cost." He produces an official-looking factory invoice. "Of course, you can't possibly ask us to take a loss on the sale, right?"

Now you feel a little embarrassed yourself. You're not quite sure how to respond. You thought you had a deal, and Fred's higher authority just shot it down. The funny part is, if you stick to your guns and talk the sales manager into meeting your price, he will eventually cave in and, congratulating you on your negotiating prowess, he will tell you that since he is selling it under factory invoice he will have to get *his* manager's approval.

This game will continue as long as you can hold out against a battalion of managers.

Understand that it is a matter of perspective. While you, as an American, may view this process as underhanded and deceptive, it is a time-honored negotiating tactic used everywhere in the world, from Middle East bazaars to Mexican street markets.

It is possible to remove the higher authority, and you should do so at

the first opportunity. When I teach negotiating to real estate salespeople, I show them how to remove the threat of a higher authority. As a salesman and his clients climb into a car, before any property has been shown, I tell the salesman to ask, "Let me understand. If we find exactly the right property for you today, is there any reason why you won't be able to make a decision?" This is not only a fairly safe question for the client—he probably won't see *exactly* the property he wants—but when he replies to the question, he may just remove the higher authority.

This is important because many people have a tendency to try to create a higher authority when pressured to make a decision, as a stalling technique. Right before signing the final papers they may say something like, "We're sorry, but we can't make a decision today because good old Uncle Henry is helping us with the down payment and we need to talk to him about it first." If the buyer has already admitted that he could make the final decision (without Uncle Henry's approval), then the appeal to a higher authority cannot be called in at the last minute.

When you enter a negotiation, before you have established any price concessions, say to the other party: "Mr. Buyer, I don't want to put any pressure on you, but I will have to have an answer today, as I have other prospective buyers, and if we can't get together on this, well, I simply can't take the chance of losing those other opportunities. So let me ask you this: If this offer meets all of your needs, is there any reason why you couldn't make a decision today?"

Again, this seems like a fairly safe question for the buyer to answer, "Yes, if it meets all my needs, then I can give you a decision tonight," because he knows that your proposal probably will *not* meet all his needs, and when the compromising begins, he feels that he is off the hook. What he doesn't realize is that you have completely removed his appeal to higher authority. He no longer has the option of saying, "I'd like to take this home and think it over," because you can always counter with: "Wait, let me go over this one more time. There must be something I didn't explain in enough detail to you before, because I know that you indicated to me earlier that you were prepared to make a decision today." Not only are you being agreeable, making it harder for him to fight back, but you have taken away his ability to stall, and that can be a very powerful maneuver. The buyer cannot fall back on the line, "Well, I did want to run it by my attorney first," because he has already admitted to you that he himself has the capability to make a decision.

If he insists that he always has his attorney approve his contracts even though he has the authority to act, you can then finish the appeal to authority once and for all with a tactic called "subject to . . ." This move is similar to what a life insurance salesman does when he's trying to sell a $100,000 policy. He might say: "Now, quite frankly, I don't know whether we can get $100,000 worth of coverage on a person your age or not. We would have to have you take a physical—at our expense, of course—which would be to your benefit whether you get the coverage or not. That's not such a bad thing, is it? So why don't I just write up the paperwork subject to the approval of the physician, and we'll set up that free physical for you." Did you catch the "subject to"?

When your buyer insists on running the contract by his attorney before signing, simply add a subject to, by saying: "Well, you may remember that I told you earlier that I was concerned about losing this other opportunity if we couldn't get together. It would certainly help the situation if we could write this up, subject to the right of your attorney to disapprove it within a twenty-four period for any legal reason." An important note here: the deal is not simply subject to the approval of the attorney for any reason he might think of; it is subject to approval or disapproval for any *legal* reason. In the case of a CPA it might be subject to any tax reason. It is subject to his disapproval for a specific reason.

I had the occasion to defuse an appeal to higher authority shortly after arriving in America in 1962. I had an interview with a large department store chain in California. The interview did not go very well and I could feel that I was not going to get the job, probably because the manager didn't believe I was planning to stay in the country. I had absolutely no intention of going back to England, yet it was plain that he didn't believe me. And so, I was not going to get the job.

He said to me, "Roger, I appreciate your coming in for the interview. I'll report the findings of the interview to the committee at the head office and you'll be hearing from them."

He was pulling the higher authority tactic, so I said, "But you will recommend me to them, won't you?" I could see him swinging between his alternatives. On the one hand, he didn't want to recommend me because he thought I would not be a long-term employee. On the other hand he hated to say straight out to me that he wasn't going to recommend me.

Finally he reached a decision, and, luckily, it was in my favor. He said, "Oh, of course, I guess I'm willing to give you a try." With that simple statement he immediately revealed that there was no committee at the head office, no higher authority, only *him*. He was the one making the decision, and he had made it in my favor.

Watch for the higher authority everywhere:

In the drugstore, where the clerk can't approve a check without calling the floor manager, who can't approve the check because it's for ten dollars over the amount of the purchase, who calls the store manager, who cites a company policy restricting him from accepting your check because your license expired yesterday.

At the garage sale, where the husband almost accepts your offer of twenty dollars on the rocking chair and then says he has to check with *the wife* because it's really her chair. He disappears into the house for a minute and then reappears with a sheepish grin, explaining that she won't consider anything less than thirty dollars, but he thinks he can get her to take twenty-five. Of course, you don't even know if *the wife* is in the house; she may be out shopping at another garage sale. But you think he's on your side.

Your opponent of a moment ago is suddenly your partner, and you find yourself saying, "Well, okay, if you think you can talk her into it, I'll pay twenty-five." He looks back at the house, then says, "Okay, I know she didn't want to go below thirty and twenty-five is just too low. Let's split the difference and make it $27.50." And five minutes later you walk away one rocking chair richer and $27.50 poorer.

If you want to use the higher authority tactic yourself, keep in mind that it is always better to have a board of directors or a committee that you have to report to, rather than a single person. It is easy to respond when the other negotiator says that their higher authority is a person. Simply say, "Well, then, let's go talk to him right now and get this thing resolved." When the higher authority is an amorphous entity it is much more difficult to deal with.

It is much easier for you as, say, an apartment owner, to form a corporation rather than let your tenants know that it is you who actually controls the property. Then, when your tenants approach you to ask for new drapes, you can say: "Quite frankly, I don't think the owners will be willing to put in new drapes at this point in time, but I'll tell you what: If you keep the rent coming in on the due date for six months, I'll go to bat with them and see what I can do on your behalf."

You should always work to keep your own resort to higher authority while removing the other party's ability to call on authority. If you do so, you'll have quite a lever at your disposal, and a great deal of room to maneuver—and that's something that should never be underestimated.

Splitting the Difference

Practically everyone has been in the position of splitting the difference. We *almost* agree; I am stuck on $200, and you insist that you won't pay more than $150. What's the solution? Let's split the difference at $175 and we can both walk away happy.

Now here's where I am going to teach an old dog (you) a new trick: *Never* offer to split the difference. Instead, always encourage the other party to offer to split the difference. This keeps you in the controlling position, and it allows the possibility of working out a split that is a little better for you than the standard fifty-fifty.

Let's imagine that in the negotiations over the price of a car you have finally talked the seller down to $8,000, while you been talked up from your first offer of $6,000 to $7,000. Perhaps the top of your negotiating range is $7,300. Should you go ahead and offer to split the difference, raising the upper limit of your range? Absolutely not. *Never* offer to split the difference. I can't stress that enough. It is so easy to see the end of the negotiation in view and say, "Well, why not split the difference and be done with it."

If you take this easy path, you're giving away a great deal of your final price. But how can you force the other person to offer the split, and how can you turn their offer to your advantage?

You should start off by stressing the small difference that separates the two offers and the amount of time that has been invested in the negotiation. When you have reached what appears to be a deadlock, you could say: "Gee, it's such a shame that we're not going to be able to put this together when we're only a thousand dollars apart. We've spent so much time trying to put this deal together, and I guess we're just not going to be able to work it out. What a shame. Of course I can find another car; the paper is full of cars

for sale, so that shouldn't be a problem. But I really thought we'd be able to make a deal here. It's really too bad, now that we're this close. Here we are within a thousand dollars of each other, and we can't seem to find a solution."

If you continue to stress how close you are, the seller will eventually volunteer, "We are pretty close, aren't we? Why don't we just split the difference?"

Congratulations, you just accomplished the first objective: get the other person to offer to split the difference. Now the game is once again turning in your favor, and you can get better than a fifty-fifty split on the difference.

You should respond with: "Let me see . . . Split the difference, huh? That would bring the price down to $7,500, right?" What have you done? You have established a new low for your opponent's negotiating range without agreeing to raise your own range one penny. He is now prepared to accept $7,500, and the range of difference is now between $7,000 and $7,500.

Now you have three choices: You can agree to split the difference; you can negotiate for a new split at $7,250 or you can agree to the split and appeal to your higher authority.

The first choice would defeat the whole purpose of the exercise, so I'll pass over it with only one comment: Stop thinking like a hurry-up-and-agree American, living in a price-tag economy. Enjoy the game and play it for all it's worth.

The second choice is weaker than the third, but you may sleep better at night if you feel guilty using the higher authority gambit. With the second method you agree that you are tempted, but you either stick to your original price of $7,000 or only raise it slightly, to perhaps $7,100. Then you play the same record over again, "It's a shame we can't agree, with only $400 between your offer of $7,500 and mine of $7,100. I really would like the car, but I just can't see paying any more for it than that. Oh, well, maybe we'll have a chance to deal again."

If you work on the $400 difference long enough, the other person will offer to split the difference again, and then he will meet the $7,300 ceiling that you put on your negotiating range.

A much more effective approach is to tentatively agree to the split at $7,500 and tell the seller that everything looks good and you'll get back with him the following morning. The next day you return and say: "I have never talked so hard in all my life. I told my partner your offer, and how you offered to come down to $7,500. But he just hung on at $7,000, and you know, I just don't know how to change his mind. It really is a shame, and I'm sorry, because I thought that today we would definitely be closing the deal. And now here we are, just $500 apart, and it looks like it's all going to fall apart on us again. How can we let this happen?"

The benefits should be clear. This gambit can bring the settlement price within your own negotiating range. Therefore, this gambit could mean the difference between making a deal or not making it.

Get Smart ... Play Dumb

In the negotiation game, smart is dumb and dumb is smart. Whenever you are negotiating, you're better off acting as if you know less than everybody else. The dumber you act, in fact, the better off you are, unless your apparent I.Q. sinks to a point of lacking all credibility.

There is a good reason for this. The justification for acting dumb is the fact that it defuses the competitive spirit. How can you fight someone who is asking you to help them negotiate with you? How can you carry on any kind of competitive banter with a person who says, "Gee, I don't know, what do you think?" Most people, when faced with this situation, feel sorry for the other person and go out of their way to help him.

Do you remember the TV show *Columbo*? It was about a detective who walked around in an old raincoat and a mental fog, chewing on an old cigar butt. He constantly wore an expression that suggested he had just misplaced something and couldn't remember what it was, let alone where he had left it. In fact, his success was due to the fact that he was being smart—by acting dumb. His demeanor was so disarming that the murderers ended up wanting to help him solve his cases because he appeared to be so helpless.

I act dumb by asking the definitions of words. A seller might say to me, "Roger, there are some ambiguities in this contract, don't you think?" And I will answer, "Ambiguities... ambiguities... hm, you know, I'm positive I've heard that word somewhere before, but I'm not quite sure what it means. Would you mind explaining it to me?" Or I might say, "Do you mind going over those figures just one more time? I know you've done it a couple of times already, but for some reason I'm not getting it. Do you mind?" And all that time they're thinking, Oh boy, what a klutz I've got on my hands this time. The competitive spirit that could have made a compromise very difficult for me to accomplish has just been laid to rest. They are not fighting me anymore, they're trying to help me, and that attitude will usually overflow into the negotiations as a whole.

The Trade-Off

In games of strategy, such as chess, it is not uncommon for one player to give up a piece, but he will do so only to gain one of the opponent's pieces or an advantage of position.

The rule of trade-off is the same in negotiating. Do not give any concessions unless you can demand a concession in return. You probably learned the rule as a child, especially if you grew up with several brothers and sisters. Jimmy could play with your G.I. Joe, but only if you could have his entire Matchbox collection for a week.

The hallmark line of the trade-off is, "If I do that for you, what will you do for me?" Use that line *every* time you are asked to make a concession, no matter how insignificant it may appear to you.

Once again, this principle has a very solid basis in reasoning. There are four excellent reasons for being so miserly in your expectations. The first is simple: you may just get something you wanted, but you are spared the trouble of having to ask for it yourself. He drops your demand on his side of the table, in essence giving you what you wanted without making you ask for it. Any last minute needs, and anything that may have been thrown out earlier in the negotiation, can now be put back into the deal for you. Even if you don't get anything immediately, you have created a situation by asking for a trade-off wherein you are the good guy, and the other side now owes you a favor.

Which brings me to the second reason for insisting on a trade-off. Remember, the more favors you do, the more points you rack up for yourself when the time of big trading is at hand. The outcome of the entire deal may

"The more favors you do, the more points you rack up for yourself when the time of big trading is at hand."

change in your favor because you helped someone else out of a bind.

The third advantage of the trade-off is the elevation of the value of the concessions. When you ask for something in return, even if the original concession you were asked to make is inconsequential, you are putting a price on the concession, making it that much more valuable.

The final benefit of this gambit is the stop that it puts to the process of having your transaction ground down by requests for free concessions. It stops the other party from constantly returning to the table in order to ask for just one more thing. If they know that every time they get something they will have to give something in return, it may make them think twice about trying to get just a little bit more.

"If I do this for you, what will you do for me in return?" is not only a legitimate question, it is a powerful negotiating gambit. And you may be surprised at the answers!

Impasse vs. Deadlock

It's very easy for an inexperienced negotiator to confuse an impasse with a deadlock. Of course, the two situations are very similar, but the dissimilarities may make the difference between closing a transaction and walking away from the negotiating table without anything to show for your efforts.

While an impasse is a dead end without an exit, a deadlock is a bolt with a very complicated lock, one that may be very difficult to open. It is important to remember, however, that there is always a key to a deadlock and therefore a way out for the negotiators.

There comes a moment in most negotiations where the two parties are a good distance apart on the issues and there is a tendency to think, If we're this far apart on the price, and he doesn't want to compromise, and I've done all the compromising I can afford to do, there probably isn't much point in continuing the discussion. *Do not* leave the negotiation! There is a way to handle such a deadlock and thus save the bargaining process.

Professional negotiators employ a technique to pick the deadlock, and it's called the set-aside tactic. This entails the setting aside of contention,

"There is always a key to a deadlock—
a way out for the negotiators."

the heart of the discussion. As soon as attention is diverted from the major point of disagreement, an attempt is made to find some agreement on the smaller problems of the negotiation.

Constant arguing can be very tiresome, and momentum will be lost if you find yourselves facing a deadlock. To restore the momentum, a good negotiator will begin the setting-aside tactic by saying, "Why don't we just put this issue aside for a moment and talk about some of the other issues involved in the negotiation." At this point the negotiations center on the solution of minor points, a strategy most salespeople know as a "minor points close." If it is possible to find agreement on just a few small items such as whether payment will be made by cash or check, or if the cabinet of that particular machine should be walnut or mahogany, such a series of little decisions can lead up to a major decision.

This gambit is used all the time in international negotiations. One instance was when the Egyptians and the Israelis finally came to the negotiating table after the 1972 invasion. The Americans, as arbitrators, approached the Israelis and said, "Why don't you at least sit down and talk to the Egyptians? If you don't talk to them pretty soon, somebody is going to start World War Three."

The Israelis' answer was, in effect: "We might be willing to talk to the Egyptians, but we want them and you to understand that one thing is completely non-negotiable here: the Sinai. We captured the Sinai desert in the war. That is where our oil fields are. We are going to put settlements there. We will never withdraw from the Sinai, and we don't care what you say."

I'm sure that you have often faced people who are that adamant when negotiating. In that situation you simply have to force down the impulse to shrug your shoulders and say, "If you feel that strongly about it, then I guess there's nothing to discuss."

When the Israelis made it so clear that they did not wish to discuss the Sinai with the Egyptians, the arbitrators returned and said: "We understand exactly how you feel about the Sinai. Goodness, that's where your oil fields are, and that's where you're building your settlements. Let's just set that issue aside for a while and talk about some of the other issues involved." At first the two parties only agreed on some minor points, but then they agreed on some points that were less minor, and before too long they reached the big issue. They found, though, that with the momentum they

"When you begin negotiating, find points of agreement
to build momentum."

had already established, with all of the minor agreements they'd reached, it was possible to resolve a problem they hadn't at first been willing to even discuss.

When you begin negotiating, find points of agreement to build momentum. Having established common ground, you can then proceed to the major points of discussion feeling that you are both working together toward a common goal – a good deal.

If you do come to an impasse – a point where neither side will give on any point whatsoever – you will be faced with two choices. The first, which almost everyone opts for, is to give up the negotiation and go elsewhere. The second option is to seek an arbitrator.

President Carter was able to be a very effective arbitrator at Camp David in the discussions between the Egyptians and the Israelis. It had taken the U.S. many years to move into a position that Egypt perceived as neutral. The movement began during the Nixon Administration, and finally, by the time Carter took office, there was something concrete for someone to take credit for.

Under President Nixon, Secretary of State Henry Kissinger took many pains to create for the United States a position of neutrality, giving the country the ability to act as a peacemaker should the opportunity arise. From the time of Kissinger's first official visit to Egypt, in 1974, he carefully established a common ground by promising aid to the embattled country.

As you can see, the choice and preparation of arbitration is not a casual decision. The future of your negotiations will likely depend on the perceived neutrality of the arbitrator. If you can find a neutral third party to resolve an impasse, you will be able to salvage a situation that would otherwise be a waste of time and effort.

I'm reminded of something I was told once, when traveling through India several years ago. I was observing a road crew busily digging a tunnel through the side of a hill. It seemed like a very primitive operation; there were thousands of workers armed with picks and shovels, and I was amazed that they would even attempt such an undertaking.

I walked up to the foreman and I asked him, "How in the world do you go about this?"

"It's very simple, really," he answered. "I blow a whistle and all the workers on this side start digging through the hill. On the other side of the

"Don't let other people give you their problems."

hill is another crew of workers, and we tell them to start digging through the hill toward us. If the two crews meet in the middle, then we've got a tunnel. If they don't meet, we have two tunnels."

The set-aside technique is like that! Something will happen, but you're never sure what.

The Hot Potato

The thick brows of the Soviet negotiator were furrowed in worry. "You don't understand how slowly the wheels of my government turn," he said. "You understand, I would be pleased to present your proposal to the party. But I don't think they will accept your proposal, and even if they do, it will be at least seven days before I will get an answer."

Now concern shows on the face of the American negotiator. His opponent has just used one of the best (and most common) middle gambits – the hot potato. Whenever one negotiator has a problem he will throw it into the lap of his opponent, trying to force the other party to solve the problem.

International negotiators have learned to test every objection for validity as soon as it is presented. This gambit is a variation on a theme – the higher authority gambit. The only way to combat the hot potato is to let the steam out of the potato immediately. You have to push back, with something such as, "If we were willing to loosen up our demands this much, then do you think we could get a response in twenty-four hours?" Test the validity of their problem and make sure it isn't just a hot potato they want to throw into your lap.

The higher authority gambit is usually used as a hot potato. When the seller tells you that he would be more than happy to sell you that rocking chair for twenty dollars but he's sure his wife won't accept your offer, you know that you have probably just been handed a hot potato. Testing his claim should pose no problem for a shrewd negotiator like you. "That's okay," you say politely. "Let's go in and talk to her, and maybe I can talk her into accepting my offer."

If the seller was sincere in his desire to accept your offer, and if his wife really is stuck on her price, then you have at least removed his higher authority. Now you are dealing with the highest authority in the negotiation – his wife.

If, however, the seller was simply throwing you a hot potato, trying to squeeze further concessions out of you, you have taken away that crutch. "Oh," he says, "I think she's in the shower right now. Oh, well, maybe I could take twenty dollars.... I guess she'll never know."

Remember the car dealer who said, "This offer is below our factory invoice cost. Surely you don't expect us to lose money on the deal, do you?" He has just thrown you the classic hot potato. He has a problem: To meet your price he will have to sell the car below his cost (or so he claims). He throws that problem at you, trying to get you to assume responsibility.

What is the solution? Toss the potato right back. You could say, "I am offering what I think the car is worth. If you paid too much for it, that's your problem, but this is how much I am prepared to pay for it." Whoosh! The potato is back in his lap.

Remember the story of the husband who had spent most of the night pacing the floor while his wife unsuccessfully tried to get him to go to bed.

"I'm worried," he said. "I have a big note due at the bank tomorrow. I just can't tell the banker that I don't have the money to pay it, and I can't figure out a way to find the money. What am I going to do?"

The wife picked up the phone and called the banker. She said, "I'm sorry to call you so late, but do you remember that note that we have coming due tomorrow? Well, we don't have the money to pay for it. Good night." And she hung up the phone.

"What on earth did you do that for?" exploded the husband. "That's what I was worried about!"

His wife smiled. "I know, dear, but now it's his problem, and you can come back to bed. No use worrying about it now."

Watch for the hot potato in every negotiation. Don't ever, ever, *ever* let other people make their problems into your problems.

SUCCESS COMMENTARY

Don't Let Your Past Immobilize You

Remember the story of the alcoholic who was constantly beating his twin sons? When the boys grew up, one of them started to drink and abuse his own family. When he finally admitted himself for professional help his excuse was: "What do you expect me to do? My father was this way and this is the only thing I know."

But the other son grew up to be a very responsible individual, never experiencing a drinking problem. His explanation for his life-style? "I am this way because my father drank and beat me. I didn't want to grow up to be the same."

You choose your reaction to a given event. That's one of the toughest lessons we ever have to learn because it knocks one of the legs we use to support our carefully built theories that explain why we aren't successful. If we are responsible for our reactions then we lose the ability to blame past events for our shortcomings.

No matter who you are, even if you have enjoyed a thoroughly pleasant, relatively uneventful life, you will have had enough bad experiences to justify not reaching your potential. After all, if Mr. Ryerson had been a better fifth-grade math teacher, you would be able to add two-fifths and one-half today, and you would probably be wealthy, but when you were sixteen, etc.

Everyone has had a loved one die tragically, or watched a close friend go through a degrading experience, or had problems with family members. As we go through these trying times, it is vital to keep in mind that it is not the event itself but our reaction to the event that will determine how it will affect our lives.

There is no end to the excuses you can find for failure, and to admit, even to yourself, that you are the master of your own destiny is really cutting things a little too close for comfort. It's much easier to blame some tragic occurrence. There is no successful person who hasn't lived through personal tragedy. But that person hasn't allowed the event to rule his or her life; in fact, in many cases the event was a springboard, propelling that person into new heights of achievement.

Statistics might convince you that your problems are not unique or debilitating. Sixty percent of all women were sexually abused as children. Fifty percent of all marriages end in divorce. Over ten percent of the children in the United States are criminally beaten by their own parents or stepparents. Richard Berk, a sociology professor at the University of California at Santa Barbara, said that "uniform crime reports and a variety of other studies. . . suggest that approximately one woman in ten will be beaten in her life by a lover, husband or dear friend."

I could quote facts and figures all day. The point is, tragedy and painful experiences are a part of life; you cannot escape taking a sip from the bitter cup. Tell me a story of woe and I'll match you with one of my own.

Here is another key difference between success and failure: Successful people do not experience any less sorrow; their difference lies in their reaction. Instead of allowing self-pity to immobilize them, they pick up the pieces and go on with their lives.

CHAPTER 4
Ending
Gambits

The pawns have been removed from the board, and you are each down to a few key pieces which have been carefully positioned for the endgame. If either of you is the weaker player, the negotiations have probably already concluded, the spoils going to the stronger. If, however, you are both still even in the game, the time has come to call your ending gambits into play.

Walk-away Willpower

The first thing to keep in mind as you approach the end of the negotiation is that you can *always* walk away. If the deal is "just about wrapped up," but you are not entirely satisfied, don't be afraid to walk away. An impasse is an impasse, and unless you can find a way around it, such as using an arbitrator to resolve disputed issues, it may be time to walk away from the table.

This is the final version of the reluctant buyer/seller. If your opponent ever senses you are satisfied—that you won't walk away—you might as well sign the papers and go home. You just gave away the king—the game is over.

It has been said that animals can smell fear and people can sense desire. No matter who said it, that assessment is remarkably accurate. Can't you tell when someone else wants something? Unfortunately, once your opponent knows that you want something that he's got, you've lost your negotiating power.

I live in a perfect example. I first saw my dream house while teaching my fifteen-year-old daughter to drive. We took the car up through some of the beautiful hills in southern California, well away from the eyes of the highway patrol. Everything about the home was perfect—and it was for sale.

Several days later I presented my offer to the seller, taking pains to give the impression that I really couldn't care less whether or not my offer was even considered. This was several years ago and the seller was asking $250,000 for the house. I offered $200,000, and he was considering my offer.

Unfortunately, I made the mistake of telling my family about the house. Up to that point I had always reserved the right to make the real estate decisions, even when it involved a house in which we would live. That may horrify you, but my family trusts my judgment, and I put years of experience in the real estate market to good use when making this decision.

This time, however, I had revealed my intentions to my loving family, who proceeded to sabotage my reluctant buyer role with amazing ease. My daughter remembered where the house was located and the next day—without my knowledge—she and my wife drove up to the house. My wife knocked on the door and asked the owner, "Would it be all right to come in and look around the house? My husband made an offer to buy it yesterday, and he told us how wonderful it is."

The gracious (crafty?) owner invited them in and showed them through the house. They oohed and aahed over every feature, and by the time they were through with the tour my reluctant buyer plan was demolished.

I have traveled quite a bit and have enjoyed several tours, some of them quite expensive (Hearst Castle, in California, runs about fifteen dollars). But my wife and daughter put me to shame when it comes to expensive tours. I've calculated that their one tour of that house cost at least $30,000.

You have to be able to walk away at any time. What happens at that point is up to the other side. Southern Californians love to practice their negotiating skills in Tijuana, Mexico, where the street vendors will haggle over every item they sell. If you have spent some time negotiating and have reached what seems to be an impasse, try walking out of the shop. The shopkeeper will usually have been simply testing your desire by throwing up a false impasse. If you're willing to walk away without that piñata or bullwhip they will run after you, suddenly willing to lower their negotiating

"If you want to buy it for a low price, don't fall in love with it."

range. You may have to walk out two or three times before striking a good bargain—and then find the same item for less at the next shop.

Leaving the negotiations does not mean they're over. In fact, they may have just begun. Many times, walking away at a crucial moment will be the only way to accomplish your objectives.

Good Guy/Bad Guy

This technique is much older than the detectives that use it in every movie. Charles Dickens used the tactic in his book, *Great Expectations*. In the opening scene of the story, the young hero, Pip, is in the graveyard when out of the sinister mist comes a large, very frightened man. This man is a convict, and he has chains around his legs. He asks Pip to go into the village and bring back food and a file, so he can remove the chains. The convict has a dilemma, however. He wants to scare the child into doing as he's asked, yet he must not put so much pressure on Pip that he'll be frozen in place or will simply bolt into town to tell the constable.

The solution to the convict's problem is to use the good guy/bad guy gambit. Taking some liberty with the original work, what the convict says, in effect, is: "You know, Pip, I like you, and I would never do anything to hurt you. But I have to tell you that waiting out there in the mist is a friend of mine, and he can be rather violent. He likes to tear little boys' hearts out and eat them, and their livers, too, and I'm the only one that can control him. But if I don't get these chains off—if you don't help me get them off—then my friend might come after you. So you have to help me. Do you understand?"

After facing the bad guy in a negotiation, it is a pleasure to feel that someone is on your side when the good guy stands up for you or apologizes for his partner's behavior. But keep in mind whose side the good guy is on before handing the reins over to him.

Think of a prospective buyer negotiating to buy a car from a husband and wife. Everything seems to be going along fine and the buyer can already envision driving away in his new car, when suddenly one of them, maybe the husband, starts to get angry and says, "I don't think this joker is serious

"Always be prepared to walk away."

about buying the car. In fact, I think we're just wasting our time here, and I've had it with this." Ignoring your embarrassed protestations he stomps out of the room, leaving you and his wife facing each other with nothing to say.

As you dejectedly start packing up all your papers, thinking that you've ruined the whole transaction, the wife suddenly says: "Sometimes he gets that way. . . . Maybe I can talk some sense into him. Why don't you let me see what I can do with him? If you're prepared to be a little more flexible, maybe we can still put this deal together."

If you don't understand the good guy/bad guy gambit, you are likely to fall for it, grateful that the wife was on "your side." Just who is selling the car to whom?

In professional business, every tactic is called into play at one time or another. When I was the president of the real estate company in California, we had one branch that consistently did not yield a profit. The branch had been open about a year. I had just signed a three-year lease on the premises, so we would be there for a while, but no matter how hard I tried, I couldn't find a way to either increase the income or decrease the expenses of that office.

The biggest problem was the lease. We were paying $1,700 a month, and that one expense was what was really killing our profit.

I called the landlord and explained my problem to him. He was not exactly sympathetic. He said, "You've got two more years on that lease and I'm afraid you're just going to have to live with it." I used every tactic I could think of, and nothing would budge him. It looked as if I would just have to accept the situation.

Finally, however, I thought to try the good guy/bad guy approach. Several weeks later I called him at about 5:50 P.M. "Look, about that lease," I said. "A problem has come up here. I want you to know, though, that I really do agree with you. I signed a three-year lease and there's more than two years left on it, and there isn't any question that I should live with it. I'm really on your side in this, but my problem is this. . . . " And then I pulled out all the stops: I used the higher authority, the hot potato, and the good guy/bad guy.

"I have this darned board of directors to deal with, and boy are they tough!" So far so good. "I have to go in there in about a half hour and they're going to ask me if you've been willing to reduce the lease from $1,700 to $1,400. If I have to tell them no, they'll tell me to close the office."

"I'll sue!" protested the landlord.

"I know. I agree with you entirely," I said. "And I'm squarely on your side, but the problem is that board of directors I have to deal with. If you threaten to sue, they'll just say, 'Okay, let him sue. This is Los Angeles County, and it will take him two years to get into court.'"

His response demonstrates how effective the good guy/bad guy gambit can be: "Do you think that you could go into that board meeting and see what you can do for me? I'd really appreciate it. I'll be willing to split the difference and reduce the lease to $1,550, but if they won't go for that, I could drop it as low as $1,500." The technique had worked so well that he was actually asking me to negotiate for him with a board of directors that may have been fictional.

When you find yourself facing a good guy/bad guy team, make sure you talk to the bad guy personally. If he is an unseen third party, insist on addressing him face to face. Tell the good guy that since he is on your side, he probably would be willing to let you address his board of directors personally.

If you have seen the bad guy yourself, and the good guy is left behind to befriend you, as in the case of the car-selling couple, handle the problem like a hot potato. Don't let the behavior of the bad guy (which is likely to be a ruse) distract you from the important issue: the price. Deal with the good guy in exactly the same manner as the bad guy; don't assume for one moment that he or she is on your side. Continue to be polite but firm in your offers. If the good guy claims that he or she cannot make the final decision and offers to take your proposal to the bad guy, leave your offer as it stands and tell the good guy that you will get back in touch at a later date. Do not give ground simply because you are dealing with a good actor.

The Withdrawn Offer

There is an extremely effective—albeit dangerous—gambit that is almost guaranteed to make or break the deal in the final stages of negotiation. In effect, the withdrawn offer is a decision to force a decision and should

therefore be used prudently. It is a subtle technique, one that you won't even recognize as a negotiating tactic unless you are aware of it.

It is easiest to describe it with an example. A buyer in a factory has been talking to a widget salesman. The buyer needs widgets. The salesman needs to sell. The salesman offers to sell widgets at one dollar apiece. The buyer counters with 90 cents. They negotiate back and forth, eventually arriving at a tentative price of 95 cents.

Then the buyer thinks, If I could get him to come down to 95 cents, I'll bet I can force the price down another whole penny. To the salesman he says: "Young man, I'm sorry, but times are rough right now. I'm afraid that I won't be able to do any business with you unless the price of those widgets comes down one more penny, to 94 cents."

This may be nothing more than a bait, to push the price down or to at least start another round of negotiations in that direction. But the salesman isn't biting. Instead of going back to the table, or throwing his hands in the air and giving up, he merely says, "Sir, if it is at all possible, I'll do it for you. Let me refigure this thing and get back to you tomorrow."

The next day the salesman comes back, remorse and embarrassment written across his face. "Do I feel awful about this!" he exclaims. "I can't understand how this whole thing happened, but do you know, over at the factory we've been up all night refiguring the cost factors of those widgets, and we found that somebody somewhere down the line has made a mistake. I know that I told you 95 cents yesterday, but there's been an error, and the lowest I can possibly sell them to you for is 96 cents."

The buyer is looking decidedly unhappy. In fact, he looks furious. "Now wait a minute," he complains, "we had a deal yesterday for 95 cents apiece, and 95 cents is what I expect. You can't make an offer and then back down on it like that just because somebody somewhere pushed the wrong buttons on their K-Mart calculator." The 94 cent offer is completely forgotten.

The experienced negotiator would never fall for the withdrawn-offer gambit. He would once again throw the hot potato back, keeping the problem—real or fictional—on the side of the table where it originated. "Look," he might say, "why don't you go back and tell your manager that you've already given me a firm offer of 95 cents. I'll bet he would be willing to go with that price, and then we can get together again and really start negotiating. . . . It really would be a shame if we can't get together on this deal, since we're only a penny apart."

The withdrawn offer is a gamble. But it will force a decision and usually make or break the deal. Whenever the same gambit is used on you, don't be afraid to counter by insisting that the other party resolve the problem and then return to the negotiating table so you can continue the *real* negotiation.

The Decoy and the Red Herring

A decoy and a red herring have something in common: They are both used as lures in hunting. The decoy is used to lure birds within firing range by giving them a false sense of security. It diverts attention away from the real issue—the hunter and his gun. The red herring is also used as a lure. It is literally a herring fish drawn across the trail of the fox to distract the hounds before the hunt.

Both the decoy and the red herring are sneaky, underhanded, dishonest gambits—dirty pool, if you will. I would never use either of them in a negotiation, even against another professional negotiator. I feel that strongly about them. Both of them should be avoided at all costs, and both of them will be used against you at some point. What I am offering here is armor, not a weapon.

When using a decoy, the other party first raises and then elevates an issue in order to take your mind off the real issue.

Perhaps you are selling equipment to a large corporation and when you present them with your proposal the purchasing agent says, "It looks okay, but there's one thing wrong with your offer. We won't be interested unless we can get delivery by September first." This is a decoy. He really couldn't care less if you deliver it a week from his mother's next birthday but he has created an issue to divert you away from the real issue: the price.

In fact, a September 1 delivery will be quite a big problem for you, as he well knows. The factory needs at least a 90-day lead time, and September 1 is only six weeks away. Backed into a corner, you struggle to arrive at a compromise. "Let me check with my people," you say, "and see what we can do for you."

You return the next day to tell him what you already knew full well: The earliest delivery possible would be October 1. Their reply: They do want your business but the delay will cause problems for them and cost them money. They are willing to accept an October 1 delivery, but only if you are willing to shave five percent off your bid price. That's the deal, take it or leave it. The decoy has done its work.

The red herrring is the same sort of device, except it will be withdrawn at a later point in the negotiation—for a price.

The classic example of the use of a red herring came during the Korean War armistice talks. Very early in the talks the parties concerned agreed that each side would be represented at the table by officials of three neutral countries, along with their own national negotiators. The South Korean side selected Norway, Sweden, and Switzerland as their three neutral negotiators. The North Koreans chose Poland and Czechoslovakia but couldn't seem to decide on the third. They suggested that the talks commence and they would find a third country later on in the negotiations.

What they were actually doing was leaving an opening for the red herring they were planning to introduce. When the time came and the stage was set, they announced the third country: the Soviet Union.

The international outcry was unanimous: "The Soviet Union? Now wait a minute! The Soviet Union is hardly a neutral power."

The North Koreans responded by saying that the Soviets were not directly involved in the conflict and therefore there was no reason for them *not* to be considered neutral.

The battle over the red (pardon the pun) herring was waged for quite a while, until the absurdity of the situation was obvious to everybody. What the North Koreans were doing, in addition to using a red herring, was to use a repetitive tactic that children everywhere understand.

"Dad," says Junior, "can I go to the movies tonight?"

Filled with paternal authority, the father says, "No son, I don't want you to go to the movies tonight."

"Why not, Dad?" (A hidden plea in the question.)

"Because you went to the movie last week."

"I know that, but why can't I go tonight?" (A definite plea.)

The father stands firm. "I don't want you going to the movies all the time."

"But why not, Dad? I don't understand." (In fact, it's starting to sound

83

more like a whine: "Whyyy not, Daaaad . . . ")

By the time dear old Dad has repeated himself ten or twelve times, he's damned if he knows why Junior shouldn't go to the movies tonight. In fact, his reasoning seems to have lost its validity and it's mostly a matter of pride and stubbornness.

This was the tactic the North Koreans were using to support their red herring. They continued to insist that they couldn't understand what the objection was to using the Soviet Union as a neutral party, until the objections of the South Koreans seemed as ludicrous as the demands of the North Koreans.

Just when it seemed as though the pointless arguing would continue forever, the North Koreans announced that they would give up having the Soviet Union on their side of the table, but only for a price.

It had already been agreed, early in the negotiations, that neither side would rebuild their airstrips. Realizing later that this left them at a severe disadvantage, the North Koreans decided that this was the time to use a red herring; hence, the Soviet Union as a negotiator. Now it was time to name the price: The North Koreans would concede and choose another negotiating party, but only if the South Koreans would forget about the airstrip restriction already agreed upon.

The North Koreans knew that they could never bring Russia to their side of the table; in fact, it was never seriously considered. But like a cheap magician they were able to create a bargaining chip out of thin air, using this gambit, and the South Koreans were helpless.

If you suspect a red herring or a decoy, keep your eye on the *real* negotiation and dismiss the spurious issue without giving any concessions whatsoever.

The Nibble

You've battled long and hard with the buyer and your old car is finally sold. It wasn't easy, but you are proud of yourself. You analyzed all three stages of the negotiation and planned your moves strategically. Your reluctant seller act would have captured an Oscar, and when you put the vise to his offer he immediately gave up $100 of his negotiating range. When you were $200 apart you got him to offer to split the difference, and you are thoroughly pleased with the final price, which was several hundred dollars above your expectations.

Your buyer reaches into his pocket for a pen to sign the contract, and as he does so he looks up and asks, innocently, "That does include a full tank of gas and the snow tires you told me about, doesn't it?" Gotcha! You are the victim of the final gambit: the nibble.

You are more vulnerable now than at any other point in the negotiation. You have wrestled long and hard; you're hot, tired, and bathed in sweat. Now you're walking away victorious, and your opponent suddenly grabs your ankle, pulling you back down to the mat.

That's what makes the nibble so effective. You don't want to give up your hard-won agreement, but you also don't want to give anything else away. After all, a deal is a deal, right? But if you lose everything now it means starting all over again, and, after all, a tank of gas will only cost you twenty bucks (forget about the snow tires—he doesn't really think I'm going to give those up, does he?). "Well, all right," you hear yourself saying, "I guess I could fill her up for you. And if you want the tires we can discuss a price."

One of the best nibblers I know is my own daughter, Julia. When she graduated from high school, her mother and I gave her a trip to Europe. She would be gone for five weeks with some friends from school, and she was thrilled about the trip.

She wanted more than a no-frills trip, of course. She wanted about $1200 spending money. Being an excellent negotiator, she brought a written proposal to me outlining her projected expenses to justify the spending money. I generously acquiesced to her demands without realizing that I was in store for a nibble.

She waited until only a few days before the trip (more on time pressure later) and then she approached me with a downcast expression. I asked her what was wrong. "Oh, Daddy," she said, "you wouldn't want me to go to Europe with this ratty old luggage, would you? All the other kids are going to have really nice luggage."

Had she presented the luggage demand at the beginning of the negotiation, I would have used my experience to negotiate it out and would have felt proud of myself for doing so. But I was up against a child, and they are really the best negotiators. The nibble had worked like a charm.

THE NIBBLE

Look out for the other party nibbling on your terms. When you have finally reached an agreement and the other person casually says, "You wouldn't mind throwing in this or that, would you?" make it very clear that yes, you would mind very much. Because if you give in to the nibble you will find yourself a half hour later wondering why in the world you did it. "We agreed on the terms, didn't we?" you ask yourself. "I didn't have to do that."

The most effective response to the nibble is to make the nibbler feel a little ashamed for using the gambit. Respond with your most condescending smile and say, "Now, Mr. Buyer, you have done such a great job of negotiating, and we have such a good deal going. Surely you're not going to make me give you a full tank of gas as well, are you?" Pass it off as though you never took the nibble seriously at all. And do it with a smile; there's no need to antagonize him at this point in the transaction.

The nibble can be a very effective tool for you to use against the other party, especially if you feel that you gave too many concessions in the negotiation. Smile sincerely and nibble gently, and you might get one or two concessions back.

Whether you are using the nibble or fighting it, keep in mind the most important rule of negotiating: It is best if both sides leave the table feeling like winners; if only one side will win, make sure it is the other side. You'll be better off in the long run.

You want to practice your tactics? No need to buy a new car or a fur coat. Spend this Saturday going to garage sales and yard sales and practice to your heart's content. Not only will you learn how to be a better negotiator, you will likely pick up some great deals. Then, when you're thoroughly versed in negotiating tactics, you may feel ready to tackle the professionals.

Knowing a handful of gambits won't make you a good negotiator, any more than knowing a few parlor tricks will make you a magician. For real negotiating success it takes an ability to read your opponent, to pick out the hidden messages that are constantly being sent, and a deeper knowledge of the intricacies of the entire game.

SUCCESS COMMENTARY

Forgiving and Living

I once attended a seminar given by the late Dr. Maxwell Maltz, author of the best-seller *Psycho-Cybernetics*. In fact, one of my most treasured possessions is an autographed copy of the book inscribed, "To my pal Roger." Dr. Maltz was one of the warmest people I have ever known; I still cannot comprehend the incredible amount of love he was able to give to others.

One of the things that struck me from his seminar was his answer when asked: What was the most important thing that you have ever experienced over the years? After all of his experience in the field of self-improvement, his answer was very simple: The most important thing he'd learned was the necessity of forgiving himself. He'd learned that each of us tends to forgive ourselves last—after we have forgiven everybody else.

For example, he said, if two people are involved in a divorce in which the fault lies fairly equally with both sides, six months after the partners have split up, each has forgiven the other but neither has forgiven himself. Each still believes that he or she was a failure in the marriage. Unfortunately, that feeling never goes away, and it becomes a part of the unconscious self-image.

It is certainly surprising that while most people may be willing to love their neighbor, they have difficulty loving themselves. The better your self-image, the more you'll be able to do for other people. So when we think of the Golden Rule ("Do unto others as you would have them do unto you"), be sure that you feel you deserve the very best.

We all have faults—no argument there. But we all want—even expect—other people to forgive those faults and accept us for what is good in us. Why, then, do we have such difficulty doing the same for ourselves? If you have had problems in your life, learn to put them behind you. Move forward until have completely forgotten the negative things in your past. Learn to forgive yourself and your whole life will change for the better.

CHAPTER 5

The
Information
Element

Why do countries send spies into other countries? Why do professional football teams study the replays of their opponents' games? Because knowledge is power, and the more knowledge one side is able to accumulate about the other, the better chance there is for victory.

If two countries go to war, the country that has the most intelligence about the other has the advantage. If two companies are planning to merge, the company that knows the most will usually end up with the better deal. If two salespeople are vying for an account, the salesperson who knows more about the company and its representatives stands a better chance of being selected for the account.

When I was growing up in England I knew that in the big-business world of the United States, Macy's was Gimbel's biggest customer and vice versa. It was taken for granted that these two competitive department stores in New York were each other's largest, if not best, customer. This was true because each store would buy merchandise from the other and analyze it ten ways from Sunday, trying to improve on price or advertising. They actually pay professional spies to do nothing more than shop at and evaluate the other store.

Despite the obviousness of the important role that information plays in a negotiation, most people spend little time analyzing their opponents before entering a negotiation. You wouldn't think of scuba diving without a mask, fins, and tank, and yet you will jump into a negotiation that will cost you thousands of dollars without any more preparation than a desire to buy or sell something.

If you are a home owner, think back to the time of purchase. How much did you know about the previous owners? Did you know why they were selling, and how long they had been trying to sell? Did you find out why they were asking as much as they were for their equity? Why they needed such a large down payment? Before considering obligating yourself to a thirty-year commitment, did you first find out everything you could about the sellers? Probably not. As I mentioned in chapter one, Americans push hard from the outset of a negotiation, driving for agreement. They rarely take the time or the effort to go through the information-gathering stage of a negotiation.

In my all-day seminars I have the students break up into small groups, with one group acting as the buyer and the other as the seller. They are given enough information to complete a successful negotiation. In fact, I purposely give each side discoverable strengths and weaknesses. If only half of these carefully planted tidbits of information were unearthed, a successful win-win negotiation would result.

Unfortunately, no matter how many times I drill these students and force them to take the time to find out more about the other side, very rarely does one side take full advantage of its training.

As a parent I have been through the experience of trying to entice an unwilling child to eat his peas and potatoes. One tactic that seems logical is the bribe. You cut a piece of chocolate cake and lay it on the table, licking your lips and making little yummy sounds. If your little darling will eat the few remaining peas and that glump of potatoes, you promise, a nice piece of chocolate cake will follow. Instead of eagerly attacking the peas and potatoes, your baby whines, stares, and drools over the cake, completely unable to understand that the cake is only a few peas away.

My students, representative of novice negotiators everywhere, drool over the final agreement, unable or unwilling to pay the small price of gathering the necessary information. Grabbing for the prize first, they only cheat themselves.

Many years ago I worked for a small department store in northern California that was part of a very large chain. This company had a rule stating that it was against company policy for any employee to say no to

a customer. The policy was sound, based on the convention that the customer is always right. If a clerk or manager did not feel that a customer's complaint was justified, they would transfer that customer up the customer-service ladder. If a customer kept complaining to this company without getting full satisfaction for his or her complaint, the problem would eventually work its way to the chairman of the board and the head office in Chicago.

There was once an elderly couple who had come into the store and purchased a Franklin Stove through the company's catalog. They had installed it themselves and, according to their complaint letter, the stove had malfunctioned, blackening the walls of their home and burning a hole in their carpet.

Everyone who faced this problem assumed it would be a very difficult task to satisfy this couple, so the letter made its way from desk to desk until it came to rest on the desk of the regional vice-president. The last thing he wanted to do was pass it on to the general office, so he wrote to me, requesting that I visit the couple and take some pictures to get an estimate for the damages.

I drove out to the little home in the countryside and met with this charming elderly couple. They were a very sweet, trusting pair that had bought a stove out of a catalog and then had been somewhat disappointed. The little old man showed me the wall of the house completely blackened with soot from the stove, and they showed me the large hole in the carpet where the coals had fallen and burned. I was also able to ascertain very quickly that the fault lay in the construction of the stove and not in the way they had installed it.

Fearing the worst, I began my discussion with a question I was sure they had addressed themselves many times: "Exactly what do you think our company should do for you? How can we compensate you for this?"

To my amazement the gentleman answered: "You know, we're retired and have a lot of time on our hands. The wall is a mess, but we can certainly clean it up. It's really no problem at all. However, we are concerned about the hole in our carpet. It's quite large, and we really don't have enought money to buy a whole new carpet. But if we had a scatter rug that we could put over the hole, I suppose that would be good enough."

Momentarily stunned, I asked: "Do you mean to tell me that if we gave you a scatter rug, that would solve the problem?"

"Oh, yes," he answered, "we'd be very happy with that."

So we all got into my car and drove straight to the store, where I helped them choose a beautiful rug to put over the hole in their carpet. I got them to sign a complete release form, saying that they were perfectly satisfied, and sent it off to the head office.

Several days later I received a letter from the regional vice-president, congratulating me on a fine job of negotiating. The whole thing was nonsense, of course; I had solved the problem by merely asking this darling old couple a question that no one had bothered to ask before: "What exactly is it you want?"

The lesson was not lost on me and served me well in the coming years, as I worked my way up the corporate ladder. I was able to solve problems for quite a few people who came in, simply because I bothered to get adequate information.

I used to have people come in to see me because they had bought a house through our real estate company, found out the building had some problems, and felt the house had been misrepresented. The sellers of the home had almost always moved out of the area, leaving the company—and me—to solve the problem.

I would sit my visitors down in my office, and with a large piece of paper in front of me, ask, "Please, I would like to know exactly what your problems are, and exactly what you think we should do for you in each instance."

"Well," they would say, "the light switch in the living room doesn't work." I would write on the paper, in large letters, "Light switch in living room." I would continue to ask them, until they had aired all of their grievances, carefully writing each on my paper.

When they ran out of complaints, I would draw a line across the sheet of paper underneath the last item and show the paper to them. Then I'd tell them what we would or would not do for them. What they wanted was clear from the beginning; they had laid all of their cards out, face up, and I was in the controlling position because I could decide what my response would be.

If I had worked like many negotiators, I would have said: "The light switch in the living room doesn't work? Well, how much does that cost, twenty or twenty-five dollars? I think we can take care of that." The home owners would have been in control throughout the entire negotiation, able to ask for an endless series of improvements. Every time the agent approved a repair, the home owners could have thought up two or three more. With my strategy they made all of their demands up front. Their demands were limited; mine were not.

If you want to learn about another person, nothing will work better than the direct question. In my own experience—and I'm not afraid to ask—I've only met a few people who were seriously averse to answering questions. For example, how many people get offended when you ask them, "What were you in the hospital for?" Not very many.

It's a strange fact of human nature that we're very willing to talk about ourselves, and yet we're reticent when it comes to asking others about themselves. We fear the nasty look and the rebuff to a personal question. We refrain from asking because we expect the response, "That's none of your business." And yet how often do we respond that way to others?

If you ever want to win a bet with someone, bet that you can walk up to a total stranger and get him or her to tell you what brand of underwear he or she is wearing. Of course, it will help immensely if you approach that stranger with a clipboard in your hand and explain that you're taking a survey. If people tell you things like that on the street, why should you be nervous about asking the questions you need answered in a negotiation?

Asking for more information in your dealings with others will not only help you be a better negotiator, it will also be a major factor in helping you get what you want out of life. Asking questions is a good habit to get into. Just ask. It sounds easy, doesn't it? Yet most of us are so squeamish about handing someone a question!

When you get over your inhibitions about asking people, you'll be surprised how many people are willing to help you. When I wanted to move my career in a different direction, I would think of the person that I admired most in the field in which I was interested. Then I would call him up and ask him if I could buy him lunch one day. It still astounds me how people who have spent a lifetime accumulating knowlege in a particular area are more than willing to share that information with me without any thought whatsoever about compensation.

It seems even more incredible that these experts are very rarely asked about the subjects of their expertise. Most people find experts intimidating, and so the deep knowledge that they have to offer is never used to its fullest.

What a senseless waste of a valuable resource, and all because of an irrational fear, compounded by socialization.

The direct question is not, of course, the only way to "get the goods" on your opponent. The second best source of information is other people who have dealt with the person or company in the past. Even your own competitors will come to your aid, willing to share what they know about a third party.

Some of the best questions to ask an official from another corporation concern the negotiating tactics your opponent is likely to use on you when you're facing each other across the table. Are they honest in their tactics? Have they ever backed out of a contract? Is one member of their negotiating team particularly nasty or gracious?

The same rules pertain to the smaller transactions, in everything from the purchase of a refrigerator at Sears to asking the boss for a raise. Talk to people who have dealt with the person you'll be dealing with. Find out as much as possible about their behavior in similar situations. As we learn more about personality styles you will see that this information will allow you to plan an effective negotiating strategy before you ever approach the person with whom you'll be dealing.

Another key to remember as you plumb these sources of information is that people tend to exchange information on a professional level. For example, if you were to ask a doctor about the symptoms of one of his patients, it's unlikely he would tell you. He would feel that the information was confidential. But if another doctor asked the same question, he would likely get a response.

In a real estate investment, for example, if I wanted to find out whether a prospective buyer of a certain piece of property was sincere or not, a call to that person's escrow agent would not reveal very much. However, a call from my escrow agent to the buyer's escrow agent is a completely different story. That phone call could be very valuable indeed in deciding if that buyer is honest and straightforward or if he usually squirms out of commitments.

Where and when you meet your opponent will be a deciding factor in how much information you're able to extract. Like two warring street gangs, "turf" is power, and whose turf you meet on goes a long way in determining who has more information power. When you sit down across the desk from

T.S. Throckett, president of Throckett's Sockets, *whose* desk you are sitting at may make the difference between a win and a loss.

A neutral meeting place may be best for the preliminary information gathering. If you meet over lunch one day, away from the formality and pomp of the office, you're much more likely to garner valuable information. This is the Off-the-Record Principle. "Just between you and me, T.S., what can you tell me about those sockets. . . ?"

An important aspect of gaining information is helping your source to understand that you definitely do not want to know the amount of last year's expenditures in order to hurt his company. You wouldn't dream of it! No, your only motive in asking about the average profit margin is to make the negotiations go smoother; to better understand the needs of the company so that you can help. Getting information from people is a skill, and a skillful negotiator will say, "I only need this information so that it will be easier to find a solution beneficial for both of us."

If you are working with a salesperson in a store, gather not only as much information as possible about the merchandise, but about the salesperson as well. Take control of the conversation and occasionally—between questions about the guarantees, delivery dates, and other features of the product—throw in an inquiry such as, "You seem to enjoy your work. Have you been working with the store long?"

There are three excellent reasons for your inquisitiveness: First, you will be able to establish a rapport, making you more than just another customer. The salesperson will feel more at ease and will volunteer more information. Second, you can find out important things about the salesperson, such as whether he or she is paid on a salary, per hour, or on a commission basis. Third, a salesperson generally has more ability to make price concessions than most people are aware of. If you show an interest in him or her as a person, you will be much more likely to get a requested discount.

The second factor is the most important when dealing with a salesperson. The reluctant buyer—especially the buyer who says, "No thanks. I really like it, but the price is just too high," and then walks away—is more likely to have the salesperson make price concessions to get the sale. The hourly wage earner will probably say, "Okay, whatever you want. Thanks for shopping." The next time you are buying tires for the car, try engaging the salesperson in more than just a conversation about the cost of radials.

You aren't the only one gathering information. Your opponent is constantly picking up information from you, especially if you are facing an experienced negotiator. Every word and action, the tilt of your head, even the clothes you're wearing, are clues collected and compiled—at least subconsciously—for use in the negotiation. That's why you must determine how much information you will give away before the negotiation begins. You should have prepared a *written* list of demands—an open agenda—for the other party to consider. Your open agenda should be honest and, well, *open*. The only piece of information that you must keep hidden is just how much you want something. Don't forget, as you share information, the power of reluctance.

On hidden agendas: Once again I have to address the issue of honesty. You are free to take your own position, of course; here is mine: I thoroughly disapprove of dishonesty. There is no room in a negotiation for a lie. However, total honesty—telling the other person how much you want something, or revealing your entire negotiating range at the outset of a negotiation—is foolhardy. That leaves me with the partial truth, also called the white lie. I will not tell a lie in a negotiation, but neither do I feel an obligation to tell everything.

For example, let's say you are negotiating with a widget manufacturer. He has made you an offer, in fact the offer he has made is the best you have heard yet . . . but you don't necessarily want him to know that because it would limit your ability to negotiate further. You have three choices: the whole truth, a lie, or the partial truth.

If you were to use the whole truth, you would tell the manufacturer that you have already received two other offers, both at least a nickel per widget higher than his price. That would pretty well close the deal, wouldn't it? Or you could lie, saying, "I've had two other offers, and they were both much lower than yours." Or you could use the partial truth, which would enhance your position without compromising your ethics. You could say, "Well, I've already had a couple of offers I'm considering. Let me get back to you tomorrow and let you know what I decide. "

Such a course may appear to be running right along the edge of a cliff, but you have not lied. It is the course I steer in a negotiation, and as the results produced by the alternatives are undeniably worse, I will continue to steer the same course.

Beware of the validity of information; truth is often subjective. As an

English schoolboy I did not learn that Great Britain was thrown out of India but rather that England had gracefully prepared India for independence. I was never taught that the colonists on the American continent revolted. I was taught that they were carefully prepared for independence, and that when the time was right they were given their freedom.

The same indoctrination takes place in all countries. In the United States we often hear that if Russia allowed its citizens to emigrate, all two-hundred-million Soviets would rush to the borders of freedom. This is, of course, utter nonsense. Probably ninety-five percent of the Soviet people are extremely patriotic and very proud of their country.

So, all information is subject to the feelings of the source. If you're planning to negotiate with the regional supervisor of a specific company and, in order to find out more about that person you approached his mother, you may walk away from the interview feeling that you are about to face a demigod. If, however, you interview the man's secretary—the one who has been denied a raise six times—you may get an entirely different perspective. Neither source is lying. They are simply telling the truth *as they see it*. It is then up to you to interpret their stories.

Information is especially powerful when you comparison shop and use the principle of "cherry picking." Gather as much information as you possibly can from every potential supplier or customer, then pick and choose the best each has to offer and use the information to put together a contract containing the best of each. Having a thorough knowledge of the options will allow you to bring up the specter of competition that your opponents fear. When asking for extra considerations, it helps to be able to say, "You know, Fred Smith over there at ABC company has promised me a thirty-day delivery and a five percent discount. . . . And Joe Harrison at National Company has offered an excellent guarantee—twice as long as the one you're offering . . . ." Having such facts and figures will help you put together the perfect contract.

All of this information gathering takes place *before* the negotiation starts. It's amazing how much information you can gather by asking the right people the right questions.

When I was a child in England, I loved to play the game Battleship. You can go into any toy store today and pick up an electronic version of the same game, but at the time, when World War II was in full swing, we would use a couple of pieces of paper separated by a barrier—usually a pile of books.

On our paper we would draw a graph with a hundred squares on it. Across the bottom of the graph we put the letters of the alphabet, and down the side of the graph we put numbers. Onto the graph we would draw our battleships, cruisers, destroyers, etc. Of course, our opponents couldn't see where our ships were drawn but they would attempt to "bomb" the ships by calling out the number and the letter of the square where they suspected we had hidden our ships. If they bombed your ship, you had to announce the successful bombing. The game would continue until one player had destroyed the armada of the other.

Every time we ask another question about our opponent, we're dropping a verbal bomb, trying to win the negotiating game by discovering the hidden agendas that lie beyond the barrier. Judicious questioning will uncover many facts that may win the game for the negotiator willing to take the time and effort to be inquisitive.

Information leads to contracts you can be happy with because they have been structured for good reasons, with a lot of thought and preparation behind them. Such contracts do not fall apart easily, and after they're signed, both parties usually appreciate the effort. Gathering information is a difficult, time-consuming task, but I cannot stress enough its importance. Information is power. It can lead you to an understanding of the other side, of their needs and desires, and will help you achieve what you want to achieve.

SUCCESS COMMENTARY

On Taking Advantage

My wife is a native of Iceland, a small island nation in the North Atlantic. I had known very little of her homeland until several years ago, when a cousin of hers came to visit us in southern California.

As we drove from the airport, and he was talking about his flight, I became intrigued. He had come by an interesting route and I finally asked him why his journey had been so roundabout. He told me he'd come on a free flight, given to him by Icelandic Airlines, and because of their schedules his passage had been rather strange.

"How did you get a free ticket from the airline?" I asked. His answer was fascinating. In fact, as the story unfolded, it seemed a page out of Ripley's *Believe It or Not!*

"Twenty-five years ago," he explained, "an Icelandic Airlines cargo plane crashed in the mountains of Iceland and I formed part of the voluntary rescue team that went up into the mountains to help the crew. We found the plane, saved the pilot and the crew, and then were able to locate the wreckage again so that the cargo could be retrieved as well. Icelandic Airlines appreciated our efforts so much that they offered everyone on the expedition a free ticket to anywhere the airline flew. And here I am."

"Come now," I said, laughing. "I'm not an idiot. You can't mean to tell me you were given a ticket twenty-five years ago and then last week you were able to go to the airline's office and redeem it for a trip to America. How did you prove your claim after twenty-five years? Did you have a voucher, or a letter?"

"No," he said, "no letter. But they had promised. Why shouldn't they give me the ticket?"

I had to point out the hole in his logic. "But couldn't just anyone walk in there and ask for a free ticket if that's the way they run things? Wouldn't people lie to get a free trip anywhere in the world?"

To him the question was ludicrous. Here was an idea that was literally foreign to him. "Why would somebody do that? In Iceland that is just not done."

It was difficult for me to envision. Imagine a country where nobody thought of taking advantage of anyone else. Unfortunately, we live in a country where that is an acceptable way of life. For us, business is business and morality is another subject entirely. Everyone wants to be a winner but it seems that too many of us will bend the rules to be one.

In negotiating, the point is to strive for a win/win situation—one in which everyone emerges victorious. Good negotiators take interest in the people with whom they're dealing and will go out of their way to reach a mutually beneficial conclusion. It's too bad a book like this is even necessary. In Iceland I wouldn't be able to sell one copy—nor would I want to. I'm afraid that when Iceland catches up with the rest of the world the other members of that rescue expedition will be out of luck when they appear at the ticket counter.

In this book I have tried to stress that the point of negotiating is not to come out the glorious victor, reeking with the spoils of battle. There is no point at all in getting what you want out of life if it means taking unfair advantage. You will have more success as a negotiator, but the victories will be hollow.

Don't be afraid to fight hard for what you want, but fight fair. In this country—and in most of the world—be prepared to defend yourself against every trick in the book—this book. But don't go to Iceland and ask for a free trip.

CHAPTER 6
The Time
Element

Vilifredo Pareto never studied the time element in a negotiation, and yet the Pareto Principle reveals the incredible pressure that time can put on a negotiation.

Pareto was an economist in the nineteenth century. Born in Paris, he spent most of his life in Italy, where he studied the balance of wealth as it was distributed among the populace. In his book, *Cours d'economie politique*, he pointed out that eighty percent of the wealth was concentrated in the hands of twenty percent of the people.

The interesting thing about the 80/20 rule is that it surfaces again and again in apparently unrelated fields. Studies done in business, education, and negotiating indicate that the same 80/20 holds true: Eighty percent of the business done by a sales team will be done by twenty percent of the salespersons. In elementary and high schools, eighty percent of the trouble in the classroom can be attributed to twenty percent of the students.

In negotiating, eighty percent of the concessions will be made in the last twenty percent of the time available to negotiate. If demands are presented early enough in a negotiation, neither side is willing to make concessions and the entire transaction may fall apart. If, on the other hand, additional demands or problems surface in the last twenty percent of a negotiation, both sides are more willing to make concessions.

Children are especially adept at using time pressure, aren't they? When my daughter Julia comes home from the University of Southern California for the weekend, she often needs money for books. When will she ask me for the money? At seven A.M. Monday, just as she's racing out the door. She'll say, "Oh, Daddy, I'm sorry I forgot to mention this sooner, but I need sixty dollars for books."

"Julia," I say, "don't try to pull this on me. I teach this sort of thing and I know what you're doing. Why didn't we talk about this earlier in the weekend?"

"I'm sorry, Daddy," she answers. "I just forgot about it until I got ready to go. Look, I'm late now and I'll have to get on the freeway or I'll be late for class. If I can't buy those books today, I won't be able to take my finals on Wednesday. Could you just give me the money now, and we'll discuss it next weekend?" She has learned the value of using time pressure.

I once conducted a seminar for the State Association of Realtors in Kalispell, Montana. I was teaching a class for the Graduate Realtors' Institute, a forum for the best and brightest of the trained agents in Montana. These students came in for an all-day course on negotiating.

At the seminar I was presenting, during one of the breaks, a lady approached me. "Perhaps you can help me," she said. "I've got a big problem. It looks like I'm going to lose a big part of my commission on a deal." As I nodded encouragingly, she explained: "A couple of months ago a man came into my office. He wanted to list his $600,000 home with me. Well, I had never listed anything that large before and I guess I didn't express as much confidence as I should have, because when he asked me how much of a commission I would charge I told him six percent. He said, 'Six percent! That's $36,000—that's a lot of money.' I told him that if he had to negotiate the price down very much, I would work with him on the commission. That's all I said, and I never gave it a second thought.

"As luck would have it, I ended up not only getting the listing but I found the buyer as well. In our business that's called a double whammy. Because of that, the entire $36,000 comission was due to me alone.

"You can imagine how happy I was, until the seller came to see me. The transaction is due to close next week, and he wandered into my office yesterday and said, 'Do you remember the deal we made before? You told me that you would work with me on the commission?'

"I said yes, very cautiously, because I wasn't sure what he was getting

at yet. He said, 'I've been thinking of the amount of work you had to do on the sale, and I've decided that $5,000 would be an adequate commission for you.' That man wanted to cut my commission from $36,000 to $5,000 – just like that! Now I've found a buyer for him and I'm afraid there's nothing I can do."

There is a basic rule that applies to any exchange of money for services: The value of services tends to diminish rapidly after those services have been provided. When the seller needed the services of an agent, $36,000 was not entirely unsatisfactory. Once the seller's problem had been solved, the same sum seemed like an enormous amount of money.

Plumbers know this principle well, don't they? They know that they are better off negotiating the price before they fix the pipes, rather than after all that's left of the problem is a few wet towels.

We once had a plumber come to our house. The kitchen was flooded with water, several inches deep. I dreaded calling in a plumber, as I had heard they charged more than most doctors and lawyers, but when I saw the mice rowing out the door in a graham cracker box, I knew I had no choice.

"Mr. Dawson," the plumber said, "I know exactly what the problem is, and I can fix it for you. It will cost you fifty bucks."

I didn't feel I had a choice at that point – the linoleum was starting to peel up in the corners – so I said, "Fine, go ahead."

It took him a whole two minutes to solve the problem. I said, "Wait a minute. Fifty dollars for two minutes' work? I'm a nationally known speaker and I don't make that kind of money!"

He smiled and said, "I didn't make that much money when I was a nationally known speaker either."

Once again, the value of services performed seems to diminish very rapidly once those services have been performed. Here I was, trying to help a woman who faced the loss of a major part of her commission because she had left that detail to be resolved at the end of the transaction. This detail, which should never have been called into doubt, had been turned into a major problem, under the pressure of time.

While this story has already served its purpose – to illustrate time pressure – you probably want the outcome, don't you? In this case I was able to solve this particular woman's problem and the whole situation turned out very well.

During the negotiations I encouraged her to keep in mind the fact that, in the eyes of every party in a given negotiation, their own position always appears to be the weakest, and the opposition's the strongest. This is because each party knows what he alone stands to lose, not what anyone else has at stake.

In this negotiation we have a real estate agent who had a written contract stating she would be paid a commission of six percent of the purchase price. Why should this agent, who was actually in quite a panic, feel threatened or in a weakened position? She felt that she was over a barrel because she knew that the seller could say at any time, "I've just decided that I don't want to sell the property." He might choose to do so, certainly; but he wanted to sell, and the real issue was whether or not he would be allowed – by her – to whittle down the amount of her commission. Who was really in a position of power?

In my view the seller had tried an extremely unethical tactic, and I suggested she face the seller with an equally strong tactic. Normally I would not suggest something like this, but in this case it seemed justified. I encouraged the agent to notify the seller that a lawsuit was pending concerning the property – a legal action over the commission fees involved. This would effectively prevent the seller from selling his property until the issue was resolved. Now the seller, under the same time pressure, was suddenly amenable. She got her full commission.

Time pressure is one of the strongest forces in coercing concessions near the end of a negotiation. During negotiations at the Paris-Vietnam Peace Talks in 1968, for example, U.S. negotiator Averill Harriman was sent to Paris by Lyndon Johnson under a great deal of time pressure. It was the spring of that year – an election year – and Johnson wasn't sure whether he could run for President again. He wanted to get the treaty resolved quickly in order to avoid political damage.

Harriman arrived in Paris and rented a hotel room on a week-to-week basis. He wanted the treaty to be signed as quickly as possible. When the Vietnamese delegation arrived, they leased a villa in the countryside for a period of two-and-a-half years. They then proceeded to spend week after week discussing the shape of the negotiating table.

Did the Vietnamese really care about the shape of the table? I think it's safe to say they couldn't have given a cat's whisker about the shape of the table. But they were trying to demonstrate their position. They had been involved in the war for thirty years, and whether the negotiations took one year or five made no difference to them. Also, they were aware of the time pressure at work on the negotiator from the United States. They knew that for all intents and purposes the U.S. had a November deadline and they wanted to put Harriman under as much time pressure as possible.

These tactics turned out to be extremely effective. If you remember that election, Hubert Humphrey was supported by the incumbent President Johnson, and was running against Richard Nixon. The weekend before the November elections, just two or three days before the voting was to take place, word came from Paris: there had been a breakthrough in the negotiations. Under tremendous time pressure the United States gave up almost everything at the negotiating table.

In my seminars, as my students practice the three stages of negotiation, I impress upon them the necessity of taking the time to accomplish their goals. They often complain that the twenty-five minutes I give them is not enough to reach a satisfactory solution. My point is: Isn't any amount of time too short?

I walk around the seminar room and study the students. I have noticed that during the first twenty minutes of the negotiating period both parties are very rigid. There is no give and take; both sides try to stonewall on the issues. But after I alert the groups that there are only five minutes remaining in the session, both sides begin to realize that without some fast negotiating, the efforts of the first twenty minutes will be lost. As the time pressure mounts, it is amazing to see the concessions that are made.

There is another side to the time element. The time invested in a negotiation tends to pay off in the form of rapport. There develops a feeling of camaraderie; a sense that "we're in this together." Having spent more than a few minutes negotiating, neither party wants to walk away from the deal.

This pressure is especially effective with a salesperson working on commission. Spending an hour haggling over the price of a ring creates a pressure to make the sale. The mark-up on jewelry is incredible, so a salesperson has a tremendous amount of leeway with the price. Take your time; make the seller work for his or her commission. And then, when the transaction is almost complete, use your natural reluctance to your advantage. Tell the salesperson that you appreciate the time invested, but the prices are just too high. . . maybe you'll come back later.

If you do come back later, come back about ten minutes before closing. Time pressure at its best: It has been a long day and all Suzy Saleslady has been thinking of for the last half hour is getting home and sinking into a hot bath. Now, just when the end was in sight, she has a customer who thinks he has forever to make up his mind about that ring. "No, sir," she says wearily, "I said $350, not $250." This guy is obviously hard of hearing as well as stupid.

"Well. . ." you say, "I really love this one, but I wasn't going to spend more than $250. . ." (pulling out his wallet and opening it slowly). "What kind of cash discount do you offer?"

How much do you think you might get the ring for? I'll bet Suzy will let that gem go for about $300.

I know the effectiveness of this type of time pressure not only as a customer but as a floor manager for a department store. Loyalty stopped at about quarter to six on Saturday night. If someone came in late as we trying to get the store closed up and asked me to give a price concession here or there, I was happy to help — I would have gift-wrapped the whole store and sold it for a dollar at that point.

Once, when coming home from Las Vegas, I wanted the airline to upgrade my ticket to first class. I had a good reason for my demand: The flight on which I had been originally scheduled had been cancelled, and the airline had transferred my flight to a later time. As a result, I would not be getting home until very late, and I was tired. I needed the extra comfort.

I knew that the airline officials would be much more flexible under time pressure, so when I got to the counter I began to discuss my case, allowing the clerk to argue with me for quite a while as the line built up. I finally said to her, "Look, I'm sure your supervisor would want to approve this. Would you mind seeing what you can do for me with him?"

I could have said, "Would you bring your supervisor out here so I can talk to him face to face?" but that would have been self-defeating. If I had done that, the clerk would have gone into the back room and said, "Would you come out here and tell this guy that he can't have first class without paying for it?" and I wouldn't have accomplished anything.

With my request, on the other hand, I put the clerk on my side. She went back and probably said something like, "Would you have any problem if I gave this guy a first-class ticket, because he's holding up the line out there." The last thing the supervisor wants to do is leave his nice cozy back room and go out to the front of the line to face angry customers. I got the ticket with no problem at all.

Time has been compared to money. They are both invested, spent, saved, and wasted. *Do* invest the time to go through every step of the negotiation; *do* use time pressure to gain the advantage; and *don't* yield to the temptation to rush to a conclusion. In negotiating, time *is* money.

SUCCESS COMMENTARY

Would You Rather Be Doing Something Else?

I live in southern California and every day, as I work my way through the hopeless mass of bumper-to-bumper traffic, I see an incredible array of creative bumper stickers. The messages range from the ridiculous to the sublime. Hundreds of them proclaim that the occupant of the vehicle would rather be skiing, or sailing, or doing any number of things other than driving.

I don't know what your reaction is to these public announcements, but I say to myself, "If you would rather be sailing, I wish you wouldn't be sitting in front of me; I could get where I'm going a lot faster."

The interesting thing about these bumper stickers is that they are untrue. Those people wouldn't really rather be somewhere else; they are right where they want to be: on a southern California freeway, hurrying to get somewhere—unless they're being held at gunpoint. Every one of them, myself included, had a choice before getting into the car and turning the key. And now, here they are, congregating on a congested highway because that was the choice they made.

We all have an incredible, almost infinite range of choices every day. And we are choosing every minute. You can put this book down now or you can continue reading. It's up to you. You're still reading? Fine, but keep in mind: you made the choice.

If I were to ask you, "Would you rather be doing what you are doing right now or would you rather be sitting in a luxurious chaise longue just outside the Royal Hawaiian Hotel at Waikiki Beach with a waiter headed toward you with a tray full of ice-cold piña coladas," what would you say?

If your answer would be Hawaii, then I would have to argue that you weren't being completely honest. If you wanted to be in Hawaii right now, that's where you'd be. "Aha!" you say, "I gotcha on that one Roger, because I don't have the money to go to Hawaii, so I couldn't be there even if I wanted to."

But you could get the money, couldn't you? You could borrow it, you could have sold something to raise the money, or you could have hit some poor old lady over the head and taken her purse. The point is, you weighed the alternatives and made a choice, and here you are.

"Wait a minute," you say. "If I did go to Hawaii today instead of work, then I would be fired!" That may be so, but you also took that factor into consideration before deciding.

I am trying to emphasize the fact that you determine, every day, what you are doing and where you are doing it. You alone are responsible for your situation, and understanding this very simple fact of life will be one of the major keys to helping you be successful in life.

When I speak at real estate seminars around the nation, it is not unusual for a husband or wife to approach me alone and say, "You know, I would have invested in real estate back in 1976 and I would have been very wealthy by now, if it weren't for my husband (or wife)! He is so conservative, he wouldn't let me do it."

"That's nonsense," I answer. "What really happened back in 1976 was that you decided that rather than face the wrath your insistence on investing in real estate would cause, you decided you would rather not invest. You made the decision—not your spouse—and you are responsible for that decision." My response does not always endear me to the person who approaches me, but I refuse to accept their excuses for failure.

We are each responsible for the choices we make every day. We are responsible for the life we lead and the success or lack of success we experience. If I end up on death row, or in bankruptcy court someday, I will have to acknowledge that I am there because of the choices *I* made. The same holds true for you. Recognize now that your future will be determined by the choices you make today, and if you would rather be doing something else, then *do it*!

CHAPTER 7
What
Influences
People

Influence. Power. Control. That's really at the heart of any interpersonal situation, isn't it? In negotiating, the person with the most influence or power will gain the most concessions. If you allow yourself to be manipulated and intimidated by other people, you can only hold yourself responsible for not getting what you want out of life. If, on the other hand, you learn what influences people and how to use and counter specific methods, you can take control of any situation.

I have studied the mechanics of influences and I've been able to pinpoint eight factors of power. In every situation where one person exercises control over another, one or more of these factors have been called into play. Whether it is a drill sergeant harassing a private in boot camp or a parent trying to maintain control over an errant child, one or more of the basic eight power factors are being used.

Power has earned a pretty nasty reputation. "Power corrupts, and absolute power corrupts absolutely." Sound familiar? And yet power, in and of itself, is not inherently evil. There is tremendous power in the ocean's waves, and yet every day hundreds of eager surfers ride the towering crests. Electricity has the power to light a child's room at night, and the power to electrocute a convicted murderer. The power itself is independent of its use. The pope has power over millions of people; so did Hitler.

Power can be a very constructive force. When I talk about power, I am

YOU CAN GET ANYTHING YOU WANT

not referring to the wanton ruthlessness of Hitler; I simply mean the ability to influence other people. I want you to learn to use power to build, and to help all sides in a negotiation accomplish their aims.

Title Power

Title power is the legitimate power that goes to anyone who holds a title. I think you have to agree you are always a little more intimidated by someone who has the title of vice-president, or doctor, than you are by plain old Mr. Smith. Power goes to anyone with a title the very moment that title is conferred.

For example, the moment the President of the United States is sworn into office, he (or she) receives the full power of the presidency, independent of any personal power that may have existed moments before.

What a president does with that power from that point on makes all the difference. When President Carter carried his own luggage into the White House and asked to be called Jimmy instead of James, he immediately set about dissipating all of the power that went along with his new title. He lost a great deal of his ability to influence people—and it showed.

President Reagan was the other side of the same coin. He did everything that he possibly could to emphasize the power of the title. He used the limousines, the state banquets, the helicopter rides to Camp David. . . strictly Air Force One all the way. He used his trappings of power—his legitimate power—to enhance his ability to negotiate. History has yet to judge President Reagan, but in the 1960s President Kennedy did the same thing, building his Camelot, and the world now remembers Kennedy as one of the most influential presidents the United States has ever had.

On a more immediate level, this power is very effective. Let's say that you are looking for a particular make and model of car and you're very interested in buying that car, if you can find it. One day after a round of golf, you cross the golf course parking lot and spy just the car you've been searching for. And it has a "for sale" sign in the window. As you are peering into the driver's window, trying to get a look at the mileage, the owner walks up. He tells you he is selling it for $10,000. That seems a little overpriced but

you promise to think about it and get back to him. He scribbles his name and a phone number on a scrap of paper and tells you to give him a call at the office if you're interested.

You decide that if you can get him to sell you the car, it would be an outstanding buy—you would love to have that car—but you will have to negotiate the price down to somewhere around six or seven thousand dollars. So you call him up and say, "I have an offer I'd like to present to you on your car; do you think we can get together and talk about it?"

"I'm very busy this week," he responds. "But my office is downtown. If you think you can come down, we can meet here and discuss it."

The lobby directory guides you to the twenty-fourth floor, where a secretary lets you into the penthouse suite. You are ushered in through doors bearing large, gold-engraved signs that say President.

Inside the large office the walls are covered with plaques and diplomas, all extolling the great achievements and accomplishments of the man behind the desk—the man you want to talk to about buying a car. He's on the phone as you're brought in, with his feet perched on the desk. He stands up when you enter, shakes your hand, then returns to his conversation, motioning you to a chair facing the desk. He's talking about selling some shares of stock on the Swiss Exchange and it sounds like a multimillion dollar deal. Finally, he hangs up the phone, smiles, and says, "Now how about the car? Let me see your offer."

How do you feel at that point about presenting an offer for $6,000? You're likely to be so intimidated that you will want to either excuse yourself politely, saying you've decided not to buy the car at all, or say, "Well, ten thousand sounds reasonable to me." At that point you wish you were buying the car from Joe the factory worker.

And yet, what does his position with a major corporation have to do with the value you place on a car? Absolutely nothing whatsoever. If the car is worth six or seven thousand dollars to you, it is worth the same whether you are buying it from a person who puts caps on toothpaste tubes or the President of the United States.

In fact, if you will analyze the situation a bit more, you have assumed that this man, a corporate president, would be unwilling to take a low offer because he is really not under any pressure to sell his car, when instead he may be much more willing to accept less money than he's asking for, because he really doesn't need the money and doesn't want to spend a lot of time getting rid of his car. On the other hand, that blue-collar worker may be under a lot of financial pressure and need every penny of the asking price of that car. Or the businessman may need cash quickly. There are many factors that should take precedence in your willingness to make an offer over the seller's position in life.

Do not allow yourself to be intimidated by titles. Some titles are totally meaningless. For instance, when I first came to the United States in 1962, I came with $400 in cash; I had to get a job very, very quickly. I found a job working as a bank teller for the Bank of America in Menlo Park, California. I always look back on that hiring decision as one of the strangest of all time because I was still struggling to understand American currency. Do you realize that American coins are probably the only coins in the world that have no numerals denoting their value? Try looking for a *10* on a dime or a *5* on a nickel. How is a foreigner supposed to know the value of six bits?

Nevertheless, I had managed to land a job as a teller, which was where I first experienced the amazing power associated with a title. I was struggling with a complicated transaction when a woman approached and demanded that I cash a $350 check for her immediately. I had been given a limit of $200 for cashing checks without approval and I told her so.

"Do you know who I am?" she stormed. "My uncle is the vice-president of the Bank of America!"

I was aware that the Bank of America was the largest bank in the world and that it had five or six hundred branches, so I was immediately intimidated by this information. But I took the standard Nuremburg defense anyway, which is to say, "I'm sorry, but I'm just doing my job."

The woman huffed off, spitting complaints about me to the officers of the bank. I could see my job flying out the window, and I whispered to the teller standing next to me, "I just got myself into a lot of trouble. I just insulted the niece of the vice-president of this bank."

The other teller laughed and laughed. "Do you have any idea how many vice-presidents the Bank of America has?" He showed me the directory of vice-presidents and it was about one inch thick. There are hundreds of branches, and every office has a vice-president. That was the day I overcame my fear of titles.

Don't forget, however, that there is power in title. While you should not allow yourself to be intimidated, you should have a title yourself. If you don't have a title at work, start a company of your own. That may seem like a long way to go to influence people, but having a company of your own will allow you to accomplish many of your goals. If you've been thinking about starting a business venture—maybe you want to sell crafts at a local fair—why not form a one-person company to do it?

I've done some research in this area and I've discovered that in most states it doesn't take all that much work or money to form a company. As I have traveled around the country, I've found that the laws don't vary much when it comes to starting a new company. Under California law, you must select a name for your company and then have a local newspaper publish an announcement stating your intention to "do business as" a named entity (called a D.B.A.), such as ABC Company. You must have this statement published once a week for three weeks and then file that name with the county recorder. The entire process, including the advertisement and the filing of necessary legal documents, costs about thirty dollars. The next step is the fun one. Appoint yourself president of the company. That's it: the power of a self-conferred title and the right to impress and influence anyone with whom you deal.

Reward Power

About half the power that a parent has over a child is reward power—also called "lollipop power." Any time one person has the power to reward another, he or she has reward power.

In the television series M*A*S*H, who had the most reward power in camp? Not Colonel Blake; it was Radar O'Reilly, as the supply officer, who had the power to hand out the goodies. Your boss has the power to reward you with raises and bonuses; your spouse may have other rewards to offer. But in every case where someone can give or withhold a reward, they have power.

Keep in mind, as you negotiate, that you often have hidden reward power. When you're shopping for a new car, you have the power to reward the salesperson with a sale, or you can withhold the sale. Even though you were the one that walked onto the car lot, keep in mind that it's *you* who will make the final decision, and therefore *you* who holds the reward power in your hand.

The only way to guard yourself from the reward power that another person has over you is to use your reluctance. Don't allow your desire for that reward to be apparent. If someone is holding your head underwater and has the power to reward you with a breath of air, hold your breath and smile; try to appear as though you couldn't care less if you ever breathe again. Make that reward appear as meaningless as possible and shrink the appearance of power.

Coercion Power

If reward power is lollipop power, then coercion power is "spanking power." It is the other half of a parent's power. When Mom or Dad threatens a child with punishment, he or she is using coercion power in its naked strength. Often its use is much more subtle; a tacit threat of embarrassment or future trouble.

You know when a state highway patrol officer pulls you off the road, as he approaches your window, he can either write you a ticket or not write you a ticket. The penalty of the ticket may not be that great but at that moment the officer has a tremendous ability to punish you, and that is intimidating.

Anyone who has the power to punish you, from a police officer to your mother, has the ability to influence you.

Punishment comes in many forms. Certainly the ticket or a parent's discipline is punishment; but one of the greatest punishments that we fear is ridicule. A negotiator must come to grips with this fear of humiliation because otherwise he will never succeed in influencing people himself. The fear of being hurt is a great influence in our lives, and there is no reason for that.

My own fear of ridicule, especially the ridicule of friends, almost got me killed. I like to ski and one of my favorite mountains is Mammoth Mountain in California. There is one run up there that's a real killer; it's called the Cornice. A cornice is an overhang of snow, formed when it is blown over the edge of a cliff by strong winds. The overhang continues to grow, finally running back down into the face of the cliff itself.

I was skiing one day with some friends who were very familiar with the Cornice and knew how to ski a cliff that steep. I had never skied it but they encouraged me to try. "Come on, Roger," they said comfortingly, "you can do it."

So, with a great deal of trepidation, I rode up to the 11,000 foot level with them on the gondola. We skied the few hundred feet to the edge of the cliff. I stood there at the top of the Cornice, looking down at the ski run. It was almost straight down for at least 3,000 feet! A skier had to go through a chute that had been cut through the top of the Cornice, so he would be skiing through snow up to his shoulders as he skied off the edge and down on the face of the cliff. From that point, if the skier made one mistake, if he stumbled on one turn, he would end up going down the entire slope on his head, with the skis clattering down right after him.

As I stood at the top admiring the fatal view, I realized I had two choices: a sure and painful death, or the ridicule of my friends if I chose to hike back up to the gondola and ride down. With that as a basis for choice, there was never a question in my mind. I don't remember how I managed to stay upright all the way down the face of the cliff—I suppose I was simply too scared to fall.

To fend off the effects of coercion power, you must overcome your fears. When the patrolman pulls you over, swallow that acidic feeling and smile. When your friends or business associates ridicule your decision, stand by it proudly and earn their respect. When the person across the table laughs at your offer, keep in mind that it's a power ploy; don't allow your fear of rejection to control you.

Life is a numbers game. There will always be people who will turn down your proposals no matter how good they are, just as there will always be people who will accept them. Let your proposals stand on their own merits and don't depend on rewards or punishments to tell you how well or poorly you are doing.

Referent Power

Referent power is available to anyone who maintains a consistent set of attractive values. The key word here is *not* reverence, although it is true that religious leaders do have quite a bit of referent power. Rather, the root word of the influence we're concerned with here is *refer*. If a person stands for something, other people tend to refer to him and treat him as an authority on that particular subject. He becomes more believable.

I had an example of this some years ago when I took a trip to Rome. An audience with the pope was arranged for me and my reaction at first was, "My goodness, Roger, you certainly have *arrived*. You're going to have an audience with the pope!" I visualized half a dozen of us international figures, gathered intimately around the pope's throne, kissing his ring and discussing the solutions to the problems of the world.

However, if you have ever been to the pope's audience hall in Vatican City, you know that audiences with the pope are an incredible affair. The audience hall holds perhaps six or seven thousand people. The pope is brought in through the back of the room, seated on a chair held on the shoulders of assistants, down the center aisle that curves through the room, then back up to a stage where he presents his message.

Flashbulbs are allowed in the hall and it is incredible to see the wave of light as they explode when he's finally seated up on the stage. I am not a Catholic, but I have never sensed greater power embodied in any one man than I felt within that man at that time. When I was able to get close to him, I was able to appreciate the tremendous ability this man had for influencing people; he is a good example of power without ruthlessness. On a physical level the pope is powerless—he is old, weak, often sickly, he has no armies or navies—and yet, on a spiritual level, he definitely has the ability to influence his listeners.

When any person is perceived as having a consistent set of values, he develops referent power. President John F. Kennedy, for example, had a definite set of consistent values. People could recognize those values and relate to them, and because of that, he was able to influence them. President Jimmy Carter, on the other hand, did not have this referent power. He was probably one of the most intelligent men that the United States has ever had in the White House (after all, you don't get to be the commander of a nuclear submarine by accident), and he was certainly one of the most personally likable presidents, yet he did not appear to have a consistent set of values. Too often he appeared to vacillate very quickly on issues, and when he did that, he lost the respect of people he was trying to influence.

President Reagan, who followed Carter in the White House, was just the opposite. Reagan had been saying exactly the same thing ever since he first ran for governor of California in the sixties. When a man like Reagan stands for something and does not deviate from that, he gains a reputation. Good or bad, he is known as a person of decision, and most people respect that. He therefore has a tremendous power to influence.

To bring this power down to earth, on a level relevant to everyday negotiations, you must learn to stick by your decisions and your values. If you are negotiating and you indicate to your opponent that you're willing to cut corners, willing to help by fudging on a loan application or avoiding a licensing fee, or doing something else you shouldn't in the negotiation, you may get a short-term gain because of your ability to put that negotiation together, but you will suffer a long-term loss in your ability to influence those people.

If you are a manager, you'll be interested to know it doesn't matter so much what your goal is or what you stand for, as long as you *stand for it.* Everyone likes to have a cause—whether or not they personally believe it is secondary.

For example, when Moses led the Israelites out of Egypt, he was leading them to the Promised Land, which in all likelihood they did not really believe in. But Moses believed in it, and he believed he was going to get there, and he communicated his convictions very effectively.

When Mount Everest was first climbed in 1953, by Sir John Hunt, many of the Sherpas who accompanied Hunt on his expedition were crucial in the effort to get to the top of the mountain, but they didn't believe for a moment that they would ever reach the summit. The Sherpas did know, however, that Sir John believed they would complete the climb and that he wouldn't give up until he had either succeeded or died in the attempt. The Sherpas followed the mountain climber because of his convictions, not their own.

In Ronald Reagan's administration the vast majority of his aides and supporters did not believe in supply-side economics, and yet they perceived that Reagan himself believed in the potential of those policies. Because of the strength of his beliefs, he was able to persuade his aides to go along

122

and give his theories a try on a national level.

Another example of a man whose beliefs were strong was John Harlin, probably the greatest American mountaineer of his generation. Climbing was his life, and at his death in 1965, at the age of just thirty years, he was attempting to climb the Eiger mountain in the Alps. His attempt differed from other, previous expeditions in that he tried to climb the daunting summit straight up the most direct face instead of taking a less challenging but safer route. After his death he was eulogized in a biography by the famed mountain climber and writer, James Ramsey Ullman. The story of Harlin's life, entitled *Straight Up*, detailed Harlin's convictions.

Straight up is a way of serving a drink. It is also a way to climb a mountain and a way to live a life. I would encourage you to live your life straight up. Learn to understand yourself and your own personal values, and then stand up for those values. Be strong in your convictions, and do not deviate from them, no matter how high the financial gain may seem at the time. The power of a reputation is indisputable, and it will last throughout your life. If that reputation calls you an honest, fair, upstanding, and considerate person, you will have an inestimable ability to influence people – and that is worth far more than any amount of money.

Charisma Power

The fifth factor of power is probably the most difficult to explain or to develop, and also the most difficult to withstand. I'm sure you have been exposed to it many times in your life, and you have probably succumbed to it. It is nearly impossible to fight against, even for a seasoned negotiator.

It is obvious that an encounter with a movie star, a well-known musician, politician, or any celebrity can leave a non-celebrity feeling a little overwhelmed. I remember an experience when I had been asked to speak on the same program as Art Linkletter. Before he began his presentation, we sat down together, just the two of us, and talked for about half an hour in the speaker's lounge. He talked about his encounters with the presidents of the last two decades, how often he had stayed in the White House, and

123

he told me about his personal conversations with them. At the end of that half hour I was almost completely under his control. If he had said, "Roger, would you please drive over a cliff for me," I probably would have done it, solely because of the power of his personality.

When meeting people who have this power, it is essential that we analyze the situation in order to recognize what aspect of that other person or his personality has given him such power. Dale Carnegie, in my opinion, gave commoners like me a great clue to the secret of charisma power in his book, *How to Win Friends and Influence People*. He encouraged his readers to treat everyone they meet in a given day as if that person were the most important person in the world; the most important person, at least, that the reader would meet that whole day.

That is a very easy thing to do with someone who might be thinking of buying something from you or might do you a favor or offer you a job, but how do you treat your taxi driver in the morning like the most important person you will meet that day? Or the waitress behind the lunch counter? Or the person you meet in an elevator on the way to your board meeting?

You have to learn to make others feel good about themselves, to feel important, without making them feel you're being condescending. If you can learn to develop this trait without overdoing it, or without your attitude being obviously phony, you will find it can be a great help to you in your dealings every day. If people feel good about themselves when they're around you, they will be happier in your company and much easier to deal with.

I remember sitting down to a meal between planes in Dallas one day along with my friend Jimmy Napier from Florida. He is a speaker on the subject of real estate investments and I have a great deal of respect for him. On this particular day he really taught me something.

Our waitress was an elderly lady who looked and spoke as if she'd been born in Italy. As she approached the table, Jimmy looked up at her with a big smile on his face and said, "Sophie [he had taken the name from her name-tag], tell me about your grandchildren."

A smile spread across Sophie's face and she said brightly, "Oh, they're just wonderful." And for several minutes she chatted proudly about the latest news of her grandchildren.

Jimmy had taken quite a chance. What if she had been offended at the automatic assumption that she was a grandmother? Or she might have been too busy to engage in any chitchat. Jimmy took the chance that she might reject his question with an "I don't have time for that, just give me your order." But he took the chance and he was able to project to her the attitude that she was important to him; more than just someone bringing in a meal. You can probably guess who got the best service in the restaurant that night. That's right—the same person who made a new friend.

There is one rule in the area of charisma power that seems to be fairly firm and clear-cut: always call people by their names. If you can see it from a name badge or from the plaque on the teller's window, or even if you have to ask for it—always call a person by his or her name. A person's own name is the sweetest music to his ears. In our depersonalized society it's always nice to think that you have been singled out of the masses and called by your *name*.

In fact, the only thing that does more for a person's ego than having his name spoken is having his name remembered. Dale Carnegie, in his memory-training sessions, used to describe the Stop, Look, and Listen approach to remembering a person's name. He used the example of the railroad crossing.

Before the railroad gates became automated there was a big sign with a cross on it, with a big light in the middle that would flash and a very loud bell that would ring whenever a train was coming near. Traffic would automatically slow down when the sign began to bang and flash and there was no need for a gate to swing down in front of the tracks. Drivers just accepted that a train was coming and stayed off the tracks.

This is a good image to place in your mind whenever you hear anyone's name. Think of the cross, the flashing light, and the bell. Think stop, look, and listen for that person's name. Use the other person's name several times in the conversation, until you become comfortable associating the name with the face. This is not a foolproof method for remembering names (someone is still working on that), but it's a good start.

Another important aspect of charisma power involves physical appearance. People who are more aware and more attentive to the way they look tend to have a great deal of personal power. Who are you more willing to discuss important matters with, the person who has not combed his hair and has horrible breath and a wrinkled shirt or the person who has taken the time to comb and wash himself?

I have known many people who were neat and clean in their dress and slobs in their work, and I have known people to be completely unkempt and even oblivious to their appearance who still perform admirably on the job. But as a general rule, neatness in appearance reflects on the complete person. The way you present yourself to others is the way they accept you and think of you. If others see you as a *mess*, you will probably have very little influence over them in negotiations.

This is not to say that you have to be gorgeous or extremely handsome; just careful about the way you appear in front of the people with whom you plan to do business. In fact, it is the attention to appearance that is valued, not the appearance itself. For this reason Lee Marvin tends to have much more personal power and charisma than Rock Hudson. Christie Brinkley's personality pales before that of Joan Rivers. Perhaps it is best to say that a good appearance may not augment a personality, but a sloppy appearance is definitely a negative.

Charisma is one of the most powerful factors of influence. It is important that you recognize those aspects of individuals who are charismatic for you and learn to incorporate them into your own personality. Through inspiring good feelings, treating the people around you in a helpful and generous way, and looking good, you will find yourself gaining in that most elusive of abilities — charisma.

Expertise Power

Whenever you're faced with someone you perceive as possessing knowledge or ability you do not have, they tend to develop the power to influence you. Doctors and attorneys are particularly good at using this factor of power. Through expertise power, many professionals have learned to ensure that their clients and patients listen to and obey their instructions. They have developed the ability to influence.

The power of expertise is not bad in and of itself. The respect that professionals gain through their knowledge is well earned in most cases, and with it individuals who are intelligent and very capable have been able to accomplish a great deal in the world. Unfortunately, the power of expertise is one of the easiest powers to abuse. Again, doctors and lawyers have done their share of this. They have created an entirely new language that sounds like gobbledygook to the average man and serves to reinforce the expertise they have that others do not. With that, many times, professionals have grabbed power that is not rightfully theirs.

The abuse of this power is easily combatted. When you feel you are on the way to being intimidated, put on your armor and start defending yourself and *your own* knowledge and abilities. Do not let the expertise of others intimidate you; use your own to gain the lead in a conversation. This power must always be used sparingly, for recently its abuses have sparked a number of defensive responses, responses that I will explain.

In the first place, do not let another person use long, impressive words on you, especially if they're out of place in the conversation or you're not equipped with Webster's latest dictionary. Often, words like that are only being tossed in to demonstrate that the speaker knows quite a few eight-syllable words.

There is no stigma attached to stopping someone and saying, "I'm sorry, but I'm not sure I understand all the implications of that expression. Could you explain it to me?" There is also the good chance that the speaker isn't quite sure of the meaning either, which could turn into a gain for you in the game of juggling for power. The chances that you will be ridiculed or lose respect because you asked for a definition of a word are much smaller than the chances that the speaker will lose face for using an expression he can't explain.

Attorneys especially come in for a lot of criticism because of their attitude toward this aspect of expertise. An acquaintance of mine, Danny Sanducci, is an attorney in California. He is very aware of the ridicule lawyers receive at the hands of the general public and often asks his clients after a hard day, "What's the difference between a dead skunk in the middle of the road and a dead attorney in the middle of the road?" He answers his own question: "Sometimes, with a skunk, you see skid marks."

The number of lawyer jokes flourishing at the moment is a good sign that attorneys have lost a great deal of respect because of their abuses of expertise power. I've had people ask me if I know how to save the lives of three attorneys. When I shrug and say that I don't, they say, "Good!" What do you have, they ask, when you see a lawyer buried up to his neck in sand? Not enough sand! they chortle.

Expertise power can be overdone, and if it is, it leads to a complete loss of respect, and consequently, power. Jokes like these are only examples of veiled ridicule. Attorneys have lost much of their ability to influence people.

Expertise power can be very advantageous to you, especially in your negotiations. If you have the element of information on your side, it can only be to your benefit to demonstrate that you do know what you're talking about. But if your presentation of knowledge that your listeners don't have is overbearing, you run the risk of losing their respect entirely. No one likes a smart-aleck.

The line between use and abuse of expertise power is a tightrope; it is very easy to fall. If you present your information by saying, "Look, let me help with this. I took a few courses on this when I was in college," chances are you will be able to demonstrate your expertise in a positive light, without putting your listeners down because they don't know as much as you do. Then you will find that your knowledge and abilities can really give you power.

Situation Power

We've all been the victim of this one, haven't we? This is the grade-school teacher who can tell you when you may and may not go to the bathroom. It's the cashier at the grocery store when you don't have enough money to pay the final bill. It's also the little guy down at the post office who might or might not accept the package you put on the counter.

At times such as these you are each face to face with a person who may be completely powerless and ineffectual in every other aspect of daily life but in that particular moment and that particular situation, that person practically holds your life in his hands. That person can accept you or reject you . . . and he doesn't even have to tell you why. Situation power gives people a great deal of influence over the actions of others, and people love to use it, don't they?

My friend Jim Tunney is a speaker from Pebble Beach, California. He told me about one of the times in his life when he was at the mercy of someone with situation power. He was the keynote speaker one night at a very formal banquet in Washington, D.C. It was a black-tie affair, and there were senators, important politicians, lots of celebrities. Jim was very, very proud that he had been chosen to be the keynote speaker.

As they were eating, he stopped a passing waiter and asked for some extra butter. The waiter said, "I'm sorry, sir, but tonight we have a larger crowd than we anticipated and I'm afraid that we only have two pats of butter per person."

Jim, rather sheepishly, said, "Excuse me, but do you know who I am? I'm the keynote speaker this evening."

The waiter leaned down and whispered in Jim's ear, "Sir, perhaps you do not understand who I am. I am the man in charge of butter."

People who work for large organizations, such as government agencies, have a working environment that is so structured that they have very little personal choice in what they do. People in these situations of little flexibility have almost no control over what they do. But whenever they are faced with a situation, however minor, in which they can exert a little control, make a few decisions, they love their newfound freedom and influence and often overplay their position. What you have to learn as a negotiator is to ignore this abuse and carry on.

When you become subject to the influence of situation power, do not aggravate the situation by challenging the other person. However difficult it may be, if you learn to let the incidents of situation power pass, you will be better off.

The dangers inherent in challenging the circumstances of situation power may be seen very often in dealing with secretaries. Often, secretaries have been given the duty to screen phone callers, and too often they take the matter of protecting the time of their employers a little too much to heart. Sometimes, they take their duties so far as to offend just about everyone who calls that office.

I'm sure that quite often the secretary doesn't realize how overzealously irritating she is. But a good salesman and a good negotiator would not let that situation get out of control by making it worse. And the situation would be worse if the next time the secretary said, "Let me see if he's in . . . may I ask who's calling?" the salesman answered, "Don't you know if your own boss is in or out? Either he's there or he's gone, and who is calling shouldn't make a difference." We all need to keep as many people as possible on our side. If that means letting the other guy enjoy a bit of control every now and again, then so be it.

Situation power can be very irritating and intimidating but it can be dealt with. Simply be courteous, understanding, and definite in your requests. If you want something, do not let someone browbeat you into submission just because they're the boss. Emphasize the importance of your proposals and your position, give your best arguments. Do not give into to situation power that has no good reasons behind it. Once you learn to handle the situation, the power that you have will surprise you.

Information Power

When I share information with someone, I form a bond with that person. If I withhold information from someone, I have created a situation wherein I have the ability to intimidate and influence.

Joseph Heller, the novelist famous for his book *Catch-22*, wrote another novel that helps to illustrate this point. *Something Happened* describes a man who works for a very large American corporation. He has made quite a life for himself, and when he enters a mid-life crisis, he is suddenly no longer satisfied with the way his life is going or with what he's doing.

In his office, this man sits with his desk facing the door of his boss' office, and every time the boss closes the door to have a private conversation, it makes the man very nervous. As the opening line of the book says, "Closed doors give me the willies." The man was torn apart by suspicion and questions.

I'm sure you can relate to this feeling. We've all been in situations in which we're aware of an exchange of information taking place and we're also aware that we are not welcome. I once worked for a man who did that to me all the time. We would be having a conference in his office and he would say, "Roger, we need to talk behind your back for a moment." He didn't believe in being deceptive; if he wanted to talk behind someone's back, he would be the first one to ask that person to turn around.

It's an awful feeling, being excluded. You know that something is being withheld from you, and if you understand the principles of information, you realize that it is more than just data being denied to you, it is the power to make judgments and decisions.

Large companies often do this to their employees. The corporate heads tend to develop a supply of information at the executive level that they won't share with the workers. The corporations that use the technique of organizing information at different levels understand that when information is withheld from employees, those employees are more easily controlled and less able to make decisions on their own. This ensures that upper management's mandates are unassailable, as is their control.

One of the most interesting discoveries in the area of business management in recent years has been Theory Z, the principle behind the Japanese style of management. Theory Z has demonstrated that it is actually beneficial for information to be exchanged with the lower levels in a corporation. Once workers know more about their company, it is easier for them to share company goals and be more enthusiastic in their jobs. They feel more trusted and much more important. They feel as if they're contributing something that is appreciated and will put in more effort to fill the needs of the company.

We have already discussed the positive aspects of information in another chapter, so at this point I would just like to reemphasize that, through information, it is very easy to gain control but that control may be short-lived. If the only influence you have over someone else is a piece of information you have and he does not, the moment that information is revealed your lever is gone. And if you have not been gentle with your influence—for instance, if you have used your power to degrade someone, or harm his self-esteem or his reputation—then not only will your lever be gone but so will any chance you might have had to regain it. You will never again have the ability to influence that particular person.

Information power is another of those factors of power very easy to abuse. However, its uses are tremendous . . . if you can maintain a positive, helpful attitude toward your associates.

The eight factors of power are used every day, all around us. If you have ever attended one of those weekend "transformation courses," then you have probably seen these power factors concentrated together and used with striking effectiveness, in ways you can recognize in most daily occurrences.

A transformation course, in case you have never been to one, is a learning program where you are locked into the ballroom of a hotel for a weekend or so while the sponsors of the course teach you all of those things they

132

promise—and advertise—will transform your entire life. The fascinating part of these courses is the amount of control that the trainer (the person conducting the training) is able to exercise over the students in the ballroom. That entire weekend, the trainer has complete influence over all of the people in the course, and if you quickly look down the list of the eight factors of power, you can see how he uses them to maintain it.

He has the power of the title: he's been assigned the title of Trainer, and he is respected because of that. He uses the power of rewards; his message is, "If you listen to me and do what I tell you, your life will be transformed." What more of a reward could you ask than that? He also holds the power of coercion and punishment: "If you step out of line during this course, I am going to humiliate you and embarrass you in front of all these other people." He wields his reference power by constant vague references to some consistent quality of integrity in his life, and emphasizes that his listeners may not have this quality. The trainer definitely has a very strong personality, and therefore, much charisma power. He is also very impressive in his methods of handling the group, and that gives him the power of expertise. Situation power—how can you argue with that one? If he can humiliate you because you need to blow your nose then that's about the ultimate situation power. Last but not least is the power of information, as the trainer alludes over and over again to the things that a student will eventually learn from him if he sticks to the program.

In that particular situation it is very easy to see how the eight factors of power can come into play as people struggle to control one another. It is also very easy to see how easy it would be to overcome this control. The next time you are in a situation where you feel intimidated, I urge you to run through this checklist mentally and pick out the methods your intimidator is using to control you. Once you have recognized the methods, you can begin to combat them.

In the business of negotiating, influence over other people is essential, so we will look at the other side of the eight factors of power. Remember, the methods that others use to influence you may also be used by you to influence others. If you increase your ability to influence other people, you will have come a long way toward getting what you want out of life. It is important that, as you learn to overcome the eight factors of power, you also learn to use them and to develop your own abilities to influence others.

133

In order to begin the development of your powers of influence it is necessary to know exactly where you stand in each of the areas right now. You must evaluate your present abilities; only then will you be able to judge adequately your strengths and weaknesses. Be honest as you fill out the evaluation sheet, and use it to help you to develop yourself.

A certain amount of explanation is necessary. I would like you to rate yourself on a scale of one to ten, one being the lowest and ten being the highest. As you study the evaluation sheet provided, please notice that I have asked you to evaluate your "three selves." We are all three different people. We are first and foremost what we know ourselves to be. The second self is the person that others see. The third self is the person we envision ourselves as—the perfect self.

Once again, be honest as you evaluate each of the three selves. If you feel you have a great deal of charisma power but other people just don't seem to respond to it, that probably means others do not see you as charismatic. If, at the same time, you would like to have even more charisma power than you do, mark your goal in the area of your perfect self. Your responses under charisma power might look like this:

	As I am
Charisma	As others see me
	As I would like to be

As you study the results of the evaluation, I want you to pay particular attention to four areas: title power, reward power, referent power, and charisma power. We will use especially these four areas of influence as we design a plan that can help you to increse your ability to influence others.

The reasons behind the choice of these four are easy to explain. In the first place, none of them gets its effectiveness by using the control of other people. You notice that we use reward power instead of coercion power. Reward power is much more positive and it does not depend upon the degradation of the other person. We will use referent power because it places an emphasis on gaining and maintaining a reputation based on consistent values. Unlike situation power or expertise power, its effectiveness is based

Evaluation Sheet

1. Title
As I am
As others see me
As I would like to be

2. Reward
As I am
As others see me
As I would like to be

3. Coercion
As I am
As others see me
As I would like to be

4. Reference
As I am
As others see me
As I would like to be

5. Charisma
As I am
As others see me
As I would like to be

6. Expertise
As I am
As others see me
As I would like to be

7. Situation
As I am
As others see me
As I would like to be

8. Information
As I am
As others see me
As I would like to be

1 = worst; 10 = best

on how much you can build up your own character, not by how much you can chew down your opponents. Title power and charisma power are both inarguably strong, and once again, both depend on constructive changes within you, not destructive changes in the other person.

These four factors are each powerful in and of themselves, but when they come together in a single person, the results can be astonishing, even extraordinary. When these four come together, you have a John F. Kennedy: a person with the power of a title, as every president has; the power to reward, as every president should have; the power of consistent and noble values that he and his followers can use to enhance unity; and the power of an extremely strong and charming personality. Although his presidency was short, Kennedy had so much influence that in many parts of the world he is still revered as the greatest American president.

Any combination of these factors can give you great power but it is the sum of all four that make that power nearly unassailable. You can go a long way, as did President Jimmy Carter, with the power of a title, rewards, and charisma, yet because he lacked that uniting force of the referent power, he eventually lost his ability to influence others. President Gerald Ford, on the other hand, had the title, the rewards, and the consistent set of values, but he lacked the personality to carry the rest off. He had no charisma with which to excite people. President Ronald Reagan had all four of these factors and used them well; so well, in fact, that he quickly became one of the most influential presidents that the United States has ever had. Obviously, efforts in these four areas can accomplish a great deal.

Unfortunately, it is this particular combination that can lead an immoral man to great power, as in the case of Adolf Hitler. This man, with the title, ability to reward, charisma, and a too-consistent set of values, led a whole nation to rise up, and unspeakable atrocities took place because of a program he devised. Remember, I said that it doesn't matter whether or not the followers believe in the leader's theories. As long as the leader believes in them and stands behind them firmly, the result will be the same as if everyone had the same basic philosophy. People followed Hitler because *he* was convinced.

People followed the Reverend Jim Jones, as well. When he took his "flock" to Guyana and gained so much control over them that he was able to persuade more than 900 people to kill themselves and their children, he was exercising these factors of power. Jones had the ability to tell his followers where to live and how to live and what to say and what to think and when to die—and that is the ultimate abuse of power.

I want to say once again: power is not inherently bad, but it can be abused. And when power is abused, the theory of win-win negotiating has no effect. When someone is abusing the power that he has to influence people, there is no way that both parties—or even one—can come out of a negotiation as winners. In a case where power has been abused, there are only losers.

Here are some of the other important factors in influencing people:

Surroundings. We have already discussed the importance of being on your own turf when you are trying to gain information. The same holds true during a negotiaton. If you can negotiate in your office rather than your opponent's office, you are always better off. This is the reason a real estate agent likes to put you in his car rather than let you drive your own. When the agent is driving, he has control over where you go and what you see.

I remember an instance when I needed to present a very important proposal to someone. I was going to pick him up at his office and then take him to the site of the business I was trying to sell to him. I was driving a Jaguar XJS, which is a very fine car, but it only has two very small jumpseats in the back. When I arrived at the prospective buyer's office, I was astonished to learn that he wanted to bring along one more person—so there would be three of us going to the site.

Much as I had wanted to drive him out in my car, his suggestion that we go in his Mercedes seemed like the only practical solution. Off we went, but on the way to the site the Mercedes started to overheat. As it turned out, I might as well have called it a day right there because the buyer said, "We'd probably better turn around and try this again another day."

There was absolutely no way the buyer could concentrate on the business proposition (the proposition that was driving me crazy) as long as he was worried that the engine of his Mercedes was going to blow up at any minute.

When people are in your office, however, or in your car, then you are in the position of control. You can make the surroundings as peaceful as possible in order to calm a prospective buyer, or as agitated as possible in

YOU CAN GET ANYTHING YOU WANT

order to hurry a possible seller into stating his lowest prices. Surroundings can give you an incredible amount of influence in negotiation.

Confusion. There is a power in confusion. This may sound a little silly but if I can get someone confused, then I have an ability to influence him. If the other person in the negotiations is so confused that he doesn't know what course of action to follow, there is an excellent chance that he will follow whatever course you tell him to.

For example, I am discussing a possible sale with a client and I say to him, "There are two possible options for you and they are very simple to understand. Let me explain them to you and then you'll be able to make a choice." At that moment I do not have control or influence over that other person's decision. The only thing I can do is guide him to accept one of the two options that I present to him.

On the other hand, I might say, "There are a lot of ways to go here and this can be very confusing. There are about twenty-five different options open to you and this is going to be terribly confusing for you because you're probably not used to handling it. Now, I have dealt with this sort of thing a great deal lately and I'm rather comfortable with this kind of situation because I see it all the time. But I am concerned that this is going to be confusing for you." If I can get that buyer more and more confused by presenting more and more alternatives to him, his mind will just bog down and he'll be more inclined to finally say to me, "Roger, what do you think?" At that point, I am in control.

If you think that I'm exaggerating the power of confusion, consider the amount of confusion that appeared on January 1, 1984, when the deregulation of the phone system took effect. For several weeks beforehand, AT&T had been advertising on television about the confusion that was going to occur and how difficult the whole thing was going to be. Customers were going to have to choose between AT&T and some other companies—they would have dozens of choices, and how were they going to decide? The whole thing was going to be a mess.

The strategy here was to make the situation appear to be much more confusing than it really had to be, and actually turned out to be. But the phone company did its best to intimidate its customers, and then the punch line was: Aren't you lucky? The easiest way out of this whole thing is to just sit back and do nothing, and let us take care of it for you.

As you can see, there is a great deal of power in confusion. The best defense that you have is just to keep your wits about you and don't let the other person confuse the issue so you surrender to him. When he starts sailing off on tangents, say, "I don't see how all of these details pertain to my decision. Instead of just confusing ourselves, could we get back to the issue?"

Competition. You can usually gain some influence in your negotiations if you advertise the fact that you have many options and do not necessarily need to make a deal here and now. If you point out that there is some competition for your product or services, and that you certainly don't need to worry about selling at this particular time, especially for less than you are asking, chances are the negotiations will fall more in your favor. And if you are buying, any seller finds it sobering to think that if he doesn't make you a good deal, someone else will.

For example, you could say to a prospective buyer, "I wish that I could give you more time to make a decision, I really do, but I have to ask for a decision right now because there are two other bids in on this and it's not fair to the other buyers for me to sit around and make them wait. Besides, they've really been putting on the pressure so I have to know now, because if you're going to back out, I don't want to take the chance of losing the other bids."

If you can create the feeling that there is competition out there in the minds of the people with whom you are negotiating, you will be able to influence them. They will feel much more pressure to get the deal signed and finished, in order to be sure.

Writing. As I mentioned previously, there is tremendous power in the written word. People tend to believe what they see in writing, while everyone has been cautioned not to believe everything he hears. The spoken word is suspect as soon as the vibrations have left the atmosphere. The written word seems to be more permanent, and therefore more trustworthy.

For example, the vast majority of people check out of their hotel rooms on time because of the little sign on the back of the door that says that check-out time is at one o'clock. Hotels used to have a terrible time getting people to leave their rooms on time because they just had a desk clerk explaining that the patrons needed to vacate before one o'clock. The sign is much more believable, cannot be swayed by the sincere question, "How about if I leave by two, will that be soon enough?" and is therefore much more powerful. If in doubt, write it out!

Risk Sharing. At my seminars I often make a proposal to my audiences. I tell them that I will offer to bet one million dollars against anyone else's $100,000, based on the flip of a coin. The gamblers in the audience know this is an excellent bet because to a serious gambler it doesn't matter what you bet on. A serious gambler at a race track cares less whether the horse will win as what the odds are, if the odds against it winning are better than they should be. The only thing that matters is the odds, and in the bet I offered, the odds are much better than they should be. For the flip of the coin, the odds should be even; in other words, two to one, and I was offering ten to one.

The odds were terrific, the bet was easy, and yet . . . I never had a single taker. That was because the potential for loss, the loss of that $100,000 if the taker didn't win, was too great, regardless of odds.

I explained to my students, however, that if there were a thousand people in the audience and they each chipped in $100, that as a group they would be much more likely to take that bet. They were sharing the risk.

People who are able to share the risk of a venture with others will do things they otherwise would not do. That is the heart of the power behind the syndication of real estate. Ten people who have a million dollars to invest are much more likely to invest that million dollars if they can get involved as a tenth interest in ten different projects rather than if they had to put the whole million dollars in the same investment.

The applications of this principle, when you're trying to persuade others to do something, are very simple. When you're trying to convince someone else to invest in something, your arguments become much more powerful if you can arrange the deal so that the risk is shared. You will be able to get people to do things they would not ordinarily do. And your persuasion will be even more powerful if they are sharing the risk with you—they are aware that you will fight hard because your survival rides on the deal as well as theirs.

I have seen this theory in action many times. Once I was asked to speak to a group of heavy equipment salespeople in Des Moines, Iowa. At this particular company, Vermeer Manufacturing, they make the world's finest trencher—it's the only one in the world that can cut through limestone. It is a very expensive piece of equipment, and although it is an excellent machine, the salespeople presenting it to different contractors had met with price resistance.

I explained to the salespeople that they should get the contractors together and allow them to share the risk and expense of owning this equipment. That way, an individual contractor would not have to take the full liability of owning the machinery. Then the equipment would be productive for the contractors, the company would get a better reputation for both good products and innovative sales, and everyone would benefit.

Time. There is a great advantage in getting people to invest time with you. At one time I was a recruiter for a large real estate company. It was a very competitive business because if there was one person with the potential and the know-how to become a good sales agent, he could go to work for any of about thirty companies in the area.

One of the techniques I used entailed persuading possible employees to spend time with me. In our conversation I would introduce the title of a book, and ask if they had read it. If they told me they hadn't, I would tell them about an interesting chapter and say I would really appreciate their opinion if they wanted to take the time to read it. Whenever I got someone to do this, I had received an investment of his time, he had made a commitment to me, and I had control over him. We would share the risk of the time that it took to continue the relationship.

The book I invariably gave away was one that had an inscription in the flyleaf. The inscription was fairly short, but very impressive, something like, "To Roger, in memory of all the good times we have had together, and in recognition of all that we mean to each other." I would tell the person who was taking the book how much it meant to me, and then he was obligated to bring it back—again, an investment of time. Not only that, but when he did bring back my book, I would have a second opportunity to discuss my company's program.

You can see the benefits of this sharing, this investment of time, in nearly every negotiation you will ever be involved in. For instance, imagine that you stop by a car lot one night and say to the dealer, "I like that car you have over there, the one advertised for $15,000. I'll give you $12,000 for it." The salesman would probably dismiss you as a complete flake.

But, if you stopped by that car lot every evening for two weeks, took the car out for a few test drives, and tied up the time of that car dealer for hours and hours, at the end of the two weeks he would probably be more open-minded to your statement: "You are a fantastic salesman. Let me tell you, I had no intention of buying a new car at this time, but if we can get together on the price, you've convinced me I should buy this car. I'm prepared to offer $12,000 for it."

The salesperson will remember all the time he has invested in you, and he's anxious to recover his investment by making a deal with you. This will make him much more flexible when it comes to the negotiating process.

If you can get people to spend time with you, and then share the risks of any investment, you will be more likely to arrive at a deal beneficial to you.

Identification. If people can identify with you and relate to what you are doing, you will be able to control them. With that in mind, when you are making a presentation to people you should not try to overwhelm them, you should try to make them understand your position and accept it as valid.

For example, if I drive up to the convention center in a Rolls Royce, dressed in a thousand-dollar suit, I am more likely to lose control over my audience than if I drove up in the same kind of car they drive and wearing the same kind of clothes they wear. Then they will be able to say to themselves, "I can understand this guy. He's a regular guy, just like me."

One of the big problems any speaker faces is the introduction he receives. If I don't give my introducer written instructions, I am likely to get an introduction that describes me as just a little less majestic than Caesar. An introduction such as that distances the audience from the speaker. By the time the introducer has finished listing all of the speaker's greatest accomplishments — which could take five or six minutes — a wall as thick and unbreakable as concrete has been built between the speaker and the listeners. The audience is sitting there thinking, Just who does this guy think he is? Some sort of great prophet? We'll just see about that! And the speaker has his work cut out for him.

Have you ever noticed how most speakers begin their speeches with a small joke? That is an attempt to remove some of the top layers of the wall, to close the distance again and help the audience to understand him. Humor is very helpful in narrowing the gap.

The easiest way around something like this is to simply prepare an introduction to be read. Something simple, not pompous, because no matter how hard you work after the introduction to overcome the bad impression, you will never be able to do it. So start off on the right foot, help your audience to identify with you, and you will have much more control.

It is important to remember that power is entirely subjective, not objective. In other words, power is in your mind and is not a tangible, measurable thing. You will only have power if you believe that you have power. In this game, attitude is everything.

As an example, take a look at the movie *48 Hours*, starring Eddie Murphy and Nick Nolte. The movie tells the story of a convicted criminal (Eddie Murphy) who has been released from prison for forty-eight hours in order to help a police detective (Nick Nolte). The convict has no substantive power at all. He has no money and no influence, and he is a convict who will shortly have to return to prison in order to complete his sentence.

There is a magnificent scene in the movie in which the convict walks into a redneck bar in San Francisco. You know the kind of place, the cowboy bar where patrons attack a black man on sight. Obviously, there is a threat here, but because the convict believes in himself, within five minutes of his entry he has everyone in the bar under his control.

Power is a mental force: an exercise of self-confidence. The strength behind the power that you can have will come only from within. This leads me to say a word concerning the many books about power and intimidation that have proliferated on the market for several years now. I would be hard-pressed to tell you the best book ever written about power, but I can easily tell you the worst. The worst book in this category that I have ever read tells you that you can control people by sitting with the light in the office coming from behind you, so that the other negotiator has to squint, or by seating your visitors in squishy couches and chairs that they sink into so they have to look up to you, or by keeping your associates waiting so they're intimidated.

This is a bunch of blatant nonsense. As I have tried to explain, true power is the result of a constructive inner process; you cannot accomplish nearly

143

as much by destroying others. Those things that some books teach are nothing but cheap intimidation tricks, and I only mention them so that you can see how truly laughable they are. Using those tricks, in my opinion, will only be self-defeating.

As you work on being able to influence people more, look for those abilities within. Do not make yourself a supposedly better person by making someone else worse. It just doesn't work that way. No matter how inviting some of those shortcuts may seem, they may work for a while but in the long run you will be worse off. There is no substitute for good hard work and a positive self-image. . . so go to it! The power is within you—all you have to do is find it.

SUCCESS COMMENTARY

Learn from Failure

Every country has its favorite heroes. The apocryphal stories that spring up about them soon make them more myth than man, or woman. Here in America, Abraham Lincoln is such a man. Every child learns the difficulties this great man surmounted: reading at night by candlelight; failing again and again on his way to the White House.

In England there is a similar account of Winston Churchill, another man who evinced the same tenacity and ability to learn from failure. As a young man he attended Harrow School, a preparatory school located near Oxford, just outside of London. Harrow School has a unique reputation, built upon for many centuries, based on the fact that until recently every prime minister of England had attended. Students who graduate from Harrow generally go on to attend Cambridge or Oxford.

Winston Churchill not only attended Harrow, he even stayed at Harrow for three years longer than his roommates. He would certainly have left earlier, had he a choice, but he failed the eighth grade three years in a row. Such an experience would have destroyed the self-confidence of most youngsters, but Winston was indomitable. He viewed those three years in eighth grade as the most beneficial period of his life, because he had to take the English class three years in a row. The additional education gave him a grasp of grammar and sentence construction that few ever achieve, enabling him to create literary masterpieces.

During World War I, Churchill was the first lord of the admiralty and as such he was in charge of the Dardanelles Campaign. The campaign was to be one of the greatest disasters of the war, in which many thousands of British soldiers were killed in an ill-fated attack. But Churchill didn't consider that a failure. He looked on the tragedy as a learning experience and during World War II, he became one of the world's best strategists. His multivolume work on the subject of the Second World War is today considered a classic.

145

When Churchill finally got the opportunity to lead his country, it was during a war-time government and he was appointed by the king instead of being elected by the people, as he would have liked. One of the first battles during his term of office was the Battle of Dunkirk, in which the British army was ignominiously forced from the European continent, back to the British islands. When asked about this great defeat, Churchill said, "Gentlemen, quite frankly, I find it exhilarating. With France falling to the Germans, we stand alone."

One night in 1941, Churchill was awakened from his sleep at 10 Downing Street, raced to the headquarters of the Royal Air Force at Biggin Hill and into the giant underground war room there. This was during the height of the Battle of Britain. From the giant map of Europe before him, and the position of the planes, he knew his country was in serious trouble. The German Luftwaffe was preparing for the complete destruction of the British Isles.

"How many planes can we put into the air to resist this invasion?" he demanded. "There are no more planes, sir," was the response. Every man capable of piloting had already taken a plane into the night sky and they were still as defenseless as a newborn kitten. The weight of responsibility must have been incredible, and yet, even in the face of defeat, Winston Churchill refused to succumb. The next day he stood before the British Parliament and said, "If the British Empire should last for a thousand years, this will be called our finest hour."

By 1945 the war was over and Churchill, the triumphant warrior, ran in the elections for Prime Minister—and was badly defeated by the candidate of the Socialist Party. Although now in his seventies, Churchill refused to accept this as a defeat. Eight years later he led the Tory party to victory, winning by election the post he had so long sought.

He considered it a high honor when, at the age of eighty-five, he was invited to speak to the young men attending Harrow School. How eager they must have been as they waited with pencils poised above paper. The greatest man in the Empire was to address them, to give them the wisdom garnered over an extraordinary lifetime. Indeed, Churchill must have pondered carefully what to say because if there was to be a future for the British Empire, the responsibility surely lay on the shoulders of these young men.

When the moment arrived, Winston Churchill looked out over the sea of expectant faces and he summed up the total of all his education and experience: "Never, ever, ever, ever, give up."

Never give up. Never allow failure to discourage you from achieving anything in this world you desire to achieve. Regard failure solely as a learning experience.

CHAPTER 8
Body
Language

In this chapter I would like to discuss body language. I know that people often get carried away with this subject, analyzing the every move of anyone they see. I compare this to the person who is so convinced of the value of astrology that he won't leave the house on a night if the signs aren't right. Or a person who says he can spot a murderer from the way he writes. Once I lost a job because, in my potential boss' opinion, I didn't interpret an ink blot correctly. In all of these cases I see a problem: Someone is taking an intangible, subjective thing and subjecting it to empirical theories, and when they're treated in that rigid way, these intangibles lose whatever validity they had.

I don't want to denigrate the possibilities of expression available in body language. I just want to emphasize at the beginning that everyone is different and everyone has a different kind of body language. I can only point out things to watch for, certain signs to be aware of. Use your own discretion and good judgment in determining if they are important.

Body language is only one of the many ways that human beings have of communicating, but a great part of communication is non-verbal. When I want to demonstrate this, I very often use a party trick. I walk around the room and ask someone there to tell me something without speaking. For example, a thumbs-up signal means good, while thumbs-down means bad and a shrug indicates indifference. In a crowd of fifty people I have never encountered a shortage of different gestures; and I think in a group of a hundred people, you would still be able to find that many forms of non-verbal messages.

A wink, a shake, a nod—all are examples of how much people can do and express non-verbally. However, if we get carried away, it's very easy to misunderstand these gestures. For example, women naturally cross their arms more than men. It is just more comfortable for them to sit that way. And if we interpret that movement as a sign that we're being shut out of that woman's mind every time she crosses her arms, we'll be making a big mistake. We could be misreading the situation completely.

Mistakes can run rampant in cases where you're dealing with people from other nations, with different customs. For instance, in the mainland United States a nod of the head means yes and a shake means no, but to an Eskimo exactly the opposite is true. Don't be too concerned with this, you probably won't be negotiating with Eskimos (or at least not with Eskimos unaware of the customs of the rest of the United States), but you should be aware that you can misinterpret the body language of others, just as they can misinterpret yours.

Possibly the greatest non-verbal misunderstanding of all time occurred in 1960, when the American space effort had been embarrassed by the success of Sputnik. President Kennedy decided to draw the nation together by giving the country a common goal to unite the efforts of the people. The goal was to put Americans on the moon within ten years and allow every American to participate. This could be accomplished by making everything public—everyone could share in the attempts, in the struggles, failures, and successes. The American public would be able to rally around this great goal for the next decade.

In 1969, when the astronauts finally stood on the moon and NASA control said to them from Mission Control, "What's it like up there?" more than one billion people were watching on television. The greatest communications extravaganza of all time and the astronauts' answer to the question on everyone's lips was an "A-Okay" hand gesture.

That was just fine for the millions of Americans watching, because everyone understands a traditionally American gesture like that, and everyone in the United States knew what the astronaut meant. But for the other millions of people watching on television all over the world, the gesture was com-

149

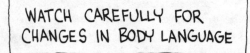

pletely misunderstood. In other nations of the world, a grown man making that gesture in public could end up in the hospital with a broken leg and several lawsuits. It's no wonder that the commentators in Japan were confused, asking each other, "What did he say? What did he say?" "I don't know," answered one, "but he seems awfully mad."

Let me illustrate the importance of body language in another way. Imagine you have arrived at the office of a friend because you have an appointment to have lunch together. You see through the glass wall of his office that he's on the phone, so you decide to wait outside. He's leaning back in his chair, with his feet propped up on the desk, and the phone is trapped under his chin. He's making a steeple with his fingers, which is generally a sign of confidence. All of a sudden his feet come off the desk, he's sitting straight up in his chair, and he starts patting his pocket, looking for a pen. He looks over to his secretary, touches his thumb to his forefinger and waggles his hand.

She knows what this means so she hands him a pen and he immediately begins writing furiously on the pad in front of him. When he has written halfway down the pad, he draws a big line under the writing, smiles widely, and marks a great big check under the line. Then he stands up, goes behind his chair, pushes the chair under his desk, and leans against it as he continues to talk.

At that point he sees you waiting in the outer office and gives you a thumbs-up sign. After saying something into the receiver he looks up at you again and holds his thumb and forefinger up, almost touching, to show you that he will only be a moment. He continues to listen, then a worried look comes over his face, and as he responds to the person on the other end of the line he touches the side of his nose — an almost sure sign that he is either exaggerating or lying. Then he reaches down, makes some further adjustments to the figures on his pad, and starts to smile again.

He reaches for his coat and has it halfway on by the time he's concluded the conversation and hung up the phone.

The point of this scenario is to make you aware of how much more you knew concerning what was going on in that office because of what you saw. You knew what was going on in the phone conversation, despite the fact that you couldn't hear either party say a word.

That's also one reason why I suggest you almost never negotiate over the phone. Always take the time to meet the person face to face, so you can watch his body language. If you're dealing with each other in person, it's particularly easy to tell if the other person is upset or agitated and you can adjust your responses accordingly.

There are worse aspects of negotiating over the phone. One of these is the fact that it is impossible to shake hands. In the United States, a handshake to settle a deal is such a powerful tool that you should never place yourself in a situation where you are unable to use it. The handshake not only gives an important sense of amiability to the meeting, it also serves to effectively seal a deal—it is a physical act of trust that can have great implications for you.

Another important thing to remember is that people are much more prone to believe what they see over what they hear. For example, if I say to you, "I'm just not going to let that worry me," and as I say it I have my hands in my pockets, my shoulders slouched, my head hung low, and an agitated expression on my face, are you going to believe I'm not worried? You would probably think that no matter what I said, I was very much worried. In that case, you would believe what you could see, not what you heard.

There are many means of communication to learn about in our study of body language. In some ways this discussion may seem very superficial, but it should be enough to get you started in learning to observe the people around you and what they're saying with their bodies.

I'd like to give you some of the most basic fundamentals you can start applying directly to the negotiating process. As we begin, I must stress that in order to learn more about body language, you must watch bodies.

There are two key places where it is extremely easy to practice your abilities at reading body language. The first of these is the airport. Waiting at an airport can be a very frustrating experience, but you can turn it into a learning experience. As you're waiting, start paying attention to people. Watch people outside your hearing range. You can see them but can't hear them. Try to interpret what they're saying, what they're doing, through their postures, hand motions, and the expressions on their faces. This is particularly challenging to try while looking at the people in a row of phone booths. Try to figure out to whom a phone caller is talking. Is it a wife, a lover, an employee? After a bit of practice you'll probably be able to figure out quite a few things about the people you're watching.

Another good place to continue your studies of body language is in your own living room in front of the television set. Turn down the sound and see what you can figure out. News commentators are particularly good for this exercise. Watch for the blinking of the eyes, the hand movements, the gestures, and you will be amazed at how much you can tell about the story they're relating.

Let's consider the uses of body language. Let's look at an actual negotiating session and see how body language plays a part. First of all, the handshake. There are many ways to shake hands. In the United States an acceptable handshake is generally described as firm, but not too strong. Most people like to give a hand several shakes.

As a rule the handshake is limited to just one hand—the right—although with a well-known acquaintance, it is not uncommon to place the left hand over the back of the other's right hand and then shake with both hands. This is considered a bit too forward for most people at the first meeting and is sometimes called the politician's handshake. A variation on the politician's handshake occurs when one person grabs the other's forearm with his free hand during a handshake. That is also considered a bit too friendly for an introductory handshake. Then again, there's the situation where one person places his free hand on the shoulder of the person he is shaking hands with; it's a sure sign that person is wanted for a committee.

Be careful with anything but a straight, firm handshake. You want to set up a feeling of friendliness, but you don't want the other person to feel you're invading his personal space or making yourself into one of his best pals for the duration of the meeting. Use the handshake as a way to meet people and make a good first impression.

As you shake hands, obviously a wet palm is considered a sign of nervousness. Look out for the person who wipes his hand on his coat as he raises his arm to shake hands.

A few years ago it was considered extremely improper for a man to extend his hand to a woman unless she first indicated that she wanted to shake hands. In today's society, however, I'm inclined to think that a man should always offer his hand to a woman in a business situation. A handshake in business becomes almost a non-verbal signal of equality and acceptance, therefore it is important to shake hands with everyone.

As soon as the handshakes are over the negotiators must sit down. Surprisingly, something as small as this may, if not properly handled, turn into a tricky situation. If you are alone and negotiating with two other people, say a husband and wife, make an effort *not* to be seated between them. If you end up with one of them on each side of you, they can exchange glances and signals to each other without your being aware of it.

When the group is somewhat larger and there are equal numbers on each side, it is typical for the two groups to sit facing each other on opposite sides of the table. If the groups are unevenly numbered, then the larger group will try to maintain that separation of forces so that the greater number on their side of the table can appear to dominate the smaller group on the other side. If you are a member of the smaller group, you will want to attempt to split up the seating arrangements so the members of both sides are interspersed. This tends to eliminate the smaller team's impressions of being overpowered.

The division of forces is particularly effective if your side is extremely outnumbered. This is because two members of the same negotiating team sitting together tend to be perceived as speaking with one voice. The negotiating team appears monolithic, solid, and extremely rigid. When the forces are divided, however, personal differences come out into the discussion. More than one opinion may be expressed and the other side suddenly loses much of its rigidity. By dividing the team you have also divided the teamwork. This might also be an advantage, if you are sitting on the now-divided larger team, because two opinions that coincide coming from two separate areas tend to give the feeling of a greater and wider support for that idea, an impression that might not be communicated if the whole team is sitting together. In either situation, it is clearly better to disperse the negotiators when one side is obviously larger than the other.

Having met everyone and seated yourself at the table, the next consideration deals with timing. When should the small talk stop and the real negotiating begin? And who will decide? As you are aware, it is very good to relieve tensions with some inconsequential chatter before the meeting starts. It is a good idea to allow everyone to relax and gather his thoughts so that everyone feels good when the negotiations begin.

There are two clear signs that every student of body language watches for as the time approaches to start the meeting. The first of these is smoking. Contrary to popular opinion, people are not likely to smoke when they're nervous. People smoke when they're relaxed. I have proven this premise time and time again. I have had a man walk into my office feeling nervous and uptight, possibly feeling that very shortly he will be in trouble—if he's not already. If I know that he smokes, I will usually continue with small talk about his family and the weather until he is feeling relaxed enough to light up a cigarette. That's when we can start discussing business.

When you have members of the team that smoke, you may sure when you see them reach for cigarettes that they're beginning to feel relaxed and comfortable enough to start the negotiating.

The other obvious sign is the coat-button phenomenon. Men will normally keep their coats or jackets buttoned up until they feel comfortable in their surroundings. If you notice during your chitchat that some of the members of the group still have their coats or jackets done up, you should keep talking. Finally, they should relax and reach down and unbutton their jackets. A survey was conducted at a wedding reception. The question was simple: the respondents to the survey were asked to decide which of the people at the reception were members of one of the two families, or just invited guests. The answers to the survey were a remarkable eighty percent accurate, because the respondents watched the coat buttons of the guests. Members of the family usually didn't button their coats at all, while visitors and friends didn't unbutton their coats until they sat down with their refreshments.

As you begin the negotiations and you are looking around the table, studying each face, try to notice how frequently each person blinks. If you have never noticed before, you will probably be surprised to notice how often people blink their eyes. Sixty times a minute is not unusual, although everyone is different, and some people may blink only once every five or six seconds.

You should collect this piece of information early on in the negotiation because you will need to use it later on, in order to notice changes in a person's blinking rate. When a person's blinking rate changes very rapidly, and the eyes start blinking very quickly, it means he or she is either very alert to what you're saying *or* under a high degree of tension and may not be telling the truth.

There's an old cockney expression in London, a slang descriptive phrase: "He's a blinking liar!" It has become accepted that most people who blink a lot are generally not telling the whole truth.

On the other hand, if the blinking rate slows substantially, you should be aware that the person is not paying attention to you and may even be dozing off, although for the moment his eyes may still be open.

The tilt of the head is also a good indication of whether a person is paying attention or not. A slight tilt to the head, especially if the tilt is accentuated by a hand on the chin, is a good sign that the person is paying attention to you. A person whose head is held straight up as he looks directly at you is probably not paying attention at all.

Speakers learn to study the head positions of their listeners. They can spot the people in the audience who are paying close attention by the tilts of their heads. If a speaker notices a large section of his audience where everyone is looking straight at him, he will work to overcome the inattention that he can see there. Often, a speaker will direct questions that require a response to that segment of the audience, or he will change the pace of his presentation in some way that he hopes will elicit more enthusiasm from that group of listeners.

Watch your audience carefully. Every time you see a hand going to the head, stroking the chin with a thumb and forefinger, you can be assured that your listeners are very alert and interested in what you are saying. Knuckles folded and under the chin reveal the same type of interest.

But when the chin goes into the hand and the whole head seems to be resting on the wrist, it's a sure sign of boredom. When you see a listener resting his head, you know that you must either enliven the presentation in order to catch his interest or prepare for snoring.

Again, I want to stress that for some people the signals commonly recognized as important in body language—such as folding the arms—are not important because those signals have been adopted as nervous habits. If a person does not normally scratch his nose out of nervousness, or does not suffer from hay fever or wear contact lenses, only then can you interpret that scratching as important. But if you *know* that that individual does not have such a nervous habit or physical problem, the things you can learn from that scratching are important. For example, a person rubbing the side of his nose as he talks to you is almost surely lying to you or exaggerating, and knowing that could be important in a negotiation.

Other movements that could be from nervousness, but more often are unconscious signals, are common. For instance, when a person tugs at his ear he is communicating to you, "I want to hear more about what you have to say." When a person scratches the top of his head, he is embarrassed or uncomfortable with what is going on, so you might be prompted to back off or change your approach.

The hands are very important to body language. We know that fingers drumming on the table indicate impatience. We also know that, under strain, many people wring their hands. Watch for steepling as well. Steepling is the term for the movement that places the two hands with just the fingertips touching and the heels of the hands separated. This is an indication of supreme confidence. If you don't believe that, just try to put your hands in that position when you're nervous. It's nearly impossible to maintain. If you see someone steepling his fingers, be aware that he feels himself to be in an extremely superior position.

When a man brings one or more hands to his chest, it is usually a sign of openness or sincerity. Don't be fooled, though; when a woman does the same thing, it generally demonstrates a feeling of shock or protectiveness. When a person touches his nose, especially if at the same time his eyes are closed, you can be fairly safe in surmising that he is concentrating very hard on what is happening in the conversation.

People really do get "hot under the collar." A hand placed at the back of the neck, whether it's a finger inside the collar or a palm rubbing at the back of the neck, almost always indicates annoyance. There is some basis in fact for feeling that people are a pain in the neck when they annoy you!

What can you tell from a person who wears glasses? Often, thick lenses can distort the expressions of a face, and if the eyes are the mirrors to the soul, glasses can hide a multitude of evils. But there are some common expressions used by people who wear glasses.

You're probably familiar with the person who looks over the top of his spectacles in order to say, "I don't believe a word you're saying" or "I disapprove of that." Someone who repeatedly cleans his glasses—and he might do it three or four times an hour during a negotiation—is similar to the person who is constantly stopping to relight his pipe. It's an indication that the person feels that he needs more time to consider what you're saying. In this position, you, as a good reader of body language, will either stop talking or talk about something inconsequential while he cleans his glasses and mulls over the more important points of the presentation so far.

Anytime someone puts anything into his mouth, whether it is an earpiece to a pair of glasses, a pencil, pen, or even a paper clip, recognize that this person is unconsciously signaling that he needs more nourishment. In other words, he likes what he hears but he wants to hear more. If someone takes off his glasses suddenly and throws them to the table violently, you would automatically realize the person is angry at something and shutting you out. That is a fairly obvious signal, but you should be aware of it, even when it is used more subtly. It means exactly the same thing when someone takes off his glasses and lays them gently on the table—the signal is just not as disruptive.

There is also the question of the space you should give a person. I have already mentioned the invasion of personal space that occurs when, on a first introduction, you shake hands with both hands or grasp the arm or shoulder of the other person. The space you give other people can help them to feel more comfortable around you and therefore add strength to your negotiating abilities. For that reason, knowing how much space to give a person is invaluable.

The study of how close you should get to another person is called "proxemics." Researchers in the field of proxemics have determined that the space within one and a half feet of a person is the "intimate zone." This zone should not be intruded upon without permission. An extended hand, a warm smile, a pointing finger are all implicit invitations into the intimate zone, an invitation that should not be taken lightly, as it indicates trust and respect.

The distance from one and a half feet away from a person to four feet is the "personal zone," while from four feet of distance to seven feet is the "public zone." The personal zone is the space that each person assigns himself for communications to one or two people—the personal zone is a semiprivate room, so to speak. Here the person converses, and where the good negotiator on a one-to-one basis might spend most of his time.

The public zone is the area the person still feels is his space—he is moving within it and can reasonably expect that space to be free from hidden obstacles to his progress. This is the sphere within which he feels safe, the area in which he is still dealing with others, though on a less personal

158

level than in the personal zone.

There are quite a few variables here, however. Every individual is different, and everyone has his own idea of his personal space. One of the determining factors for the extent of the personal and intimate zones is, not surprisingly, nationality. People who come from very crowded countries, such as Japan or England, are more comfortable in a crowded environment. Americans tend to be very uncomfortable in a crowded environment. Also, those people who come from places with high population density can shut themselves off more completely with a limited amount of space. An Englishman can be far more isolated in a crowd than an American can be because the Englishman has dealt with a great number of people around him all his life while an American is more used to wide open spaces. This all comes down to the point that you can get much closer to an Englishman or a Japanese than you can to an American before you are seen as an intruder. The same principle holds true for people raised in cities as opposed to those with extremely rural backgrounds. Los Angeles, Chicago, and New York all force their residents to adjust to a limited personal space while the countryside allows residents to extend their personal spheres to much larger proportions.

Another factor is the relationship of your size to the size of the person with whom you are dealing. If you are six feet tall and well over two hundred pounds, and you're speaking to someone who is five feet ten and weighs one hundred and fifty, the amount of personal space you allow will have to be adjusted. You should stand considerably farther from that person than you would from a person who's six feet two and well over two hundred and fifty pounds. Another way to lessen the effect of being overpowering is to stand slightly sideways as you speak with the other person, so that you do not project the image of a gigantic wall.

The old adage, "Pick on someone your own size," is extremely valid in this situation. If you stand too close to someone much smaller than you are, you run the risk of overpowering that person, hurting his self-image, and making him feel very uncomfortable around you. All of these side effects can damage your ability to negotiate with that person. On the other hand, if you stand too far away from someone considerably larger than you are, you might give the impression of being ineffectual or weak; you might even make the other person feel that *he* is intimidating *you*!

I have mentioned several times the importance of negotiating face to face, in person. Only when you can see the person with whom you are talking can you judge what he's feeling as he talks, because only then can you study his facial expressions and the movements of his body. You should keep in mind, however, that as you're learning more about the other person's feelings from his body language, he is in a position to learn more about you. This may at first seem like a disadvantage, and you should be careful with what you project through your own body language, yet the benefits should not be underestimated.

For example, when you're talking with someone over the phone and his ideas are completely unacceptable to you, it is very difficult to project how upset you may be feeling. I have often been confronted with a situation in which the other person was extremely upset and I didn't realize it because I'd spoken to him only over the phone and hadn't recognized the anger in his voice. Once, I found myself on the phone discussing something with a division manager in my company that I didn't think was a very big problem. After twenty minutes of discussion he finally said, "Well, if that's the way that you feel about it, you can expect my resignation on your desk tomorrow." I had had no idea he was even slightly perturbed, but had we been sitting face to face, I could have seen it. I would have realized that what was only a minor problem to me was very important to him. I could have noticed when he began to get uncomfortable, by the way he touched his head or the way he moved around in his chair, and knowing how important the issue was to him, I might have been able to come up with a solution to the problem that was better for him.

I began to wonder how many times I had become angry and lost a deal, thinking the person I was dealing with over the phone was just as serious as I was when that might not have been the case. How many negotiations had I lost because I hadn't been able to express my dissatisfaction adequately? From that point on I made it a rule that however inconvenient it was for me, if I had something sensitive to discuss, or some point I needed to convince someone of, that I would meet that person face to face, and not even suggest a discussion over the telephone.

As far as the practical applications of body language go, anyone who tries to read another person's thoughts through that person's motions must always be very careful. Seeing someone in person is a very powerful key to understanding how that person feels; the clues I have mentioned so far in this chapter are valid but the fact still remains that every person is different, and not every signal may mean for that person what it means for the general public.

For example, I have a chronic tension headache and because of it I rub the back of my neck a lot. That does not mean I am irritable. It just eases the pain in the back of my head. Or perhaps a person *does* tend to crave cigarettes when he's nervous, and feels no need for them when he's relaxed, and therefore walks into an important meeting with a cigarette in his hand. That does not necessarily mean he's relaxed and ready to begin negotiating. Nor is it necessarily a signal that a person whom you are sure is a smoker is still nervous because he hasn't lit a cigarette. Perhaps he recognizes there are non-smokers in the room and perhaps is abstaining out of consideration for them, or perhaps his doctor told him yesterday that he should quit.

Some people touch their noses, scratch their ears, touch their fingertips together many, many times in a day and the motions mean absolutely nothing at all. When Johnny Carson comes out on stage and says, "We have a really great show for you tonight, folks!" and scratches his nose at the same time, he's able to communicate the idea that the show probably won't be all that great. But the other negotiator's consistent rubbing at his nose doesn't have to mean he's lying. The other negotiator might just have a cold.

The key to help you determine which of the motions that you see are really important and which are not is the early observation of another person's natural habits and characteristics. It's not what the person does all the time that is important—that's habit and doesn't mean a thing in most circumstances. It is when there is a *change* in behavior that the good reader of body language should prick up his ears and be careful.

I know a fellow who is such an expert on reading body language that he's frequently asked to sit with attorneys and help them observe the witnesses in a trial, in order to judge whether or not they are telling the truth and where their weaknesses are. He clues the attorneys to the body signals of the witnesses: both to what the witnesses do habitually and what they do abnormally. He points out to the lawyers that the person who enters the witness stand with his coat unbuttoned, and his shirt untucked, is not necessarily feeling extremely relaxed in that situation. That person is probably just a slob. When the very prim and proper witness, on the other hand, unbuttons his coat three or four minutes into his testimony, *that* is, in all likelihood, a manifestation of body language. There has obviously been a change in that person's attitude, and by studying him further the implications of that change should become apparent. Once again, the important thing to notice is not what the person does normally but what he starts to do in an abnormal situation.

One of the most interesting aspects of body language appears when you're dealing with someone you know has also studied body language. In that case, you know that while you're studying him, he's studying you, and it is easily within your power to fake your feelings and project something you may not really feel in order to gain an advantage.

I think it was Shakespeare who said, "The longer the stare, the bigger the lie." For the reader of body language that means the lies that a person is trying to get away with usually cannot hold up when a person is looked directly in the eyes. He begins to crack and his honesty starts to show. People who are lying or even exaggerating tend to be very uncomfortable when looking someone else in the eyes. But people who understand that theory will be able to counter any challenge to their honesty with a simple open stare.

If you know that the person with whom you are negotiating is watching you for your body language, there are many tactics you can use to protect yourself. For example, if you have studied your own body language (a very good idea) and have recognized things you do when you're feeling at a disadvantage, you could practice those movements though an entire meeting so that the other negotiator will look on those traits as natural and not read any importance into them when you really do feel at a disadvantage.

You could also use some of the techniques for showing non-verbal disapproval when you are discussing prices, for instance, as a form of flinching, when maybe you are not that unwilling to pay as much as he's asking. But if he notices your body expressing disapproval, he may feel it necessary to squeeze his negotiating range a bit in order for it to be more satisfactory to you. You may have lowered his price without having to say a word.

Body language can be an important aspect of your negotiating techniques. The ability to accurately read the inner feelings of the people with whom you are dealing can be very helpful. I suppose, though, that the key word is *accurately.* I caution all my students that while body language may afford valuable clues, the pieces of information that can be gleaned by it are only clues. And I have by no means written a definitive study of body language. You should never *depend* upon body lanuage when you are negotiating. Use it, let it help you to get what you want out of a negotiation and also to read the needs of the other parties in the negotiation so that a win-win solution becomes more possible. If body language is used carefully, with a great deal of common sense, you should be quite pleased with the results.

SUCCESS COMMENTARY

Life is Neutral

When I was growing up in England, one of the most popular books of the day was entitled *The Jungle is Neutral*. It was written by a British soldier named Fred Spencer, who was garrisoned in Singapore during World War II.

Singapore is a tiny island country off the Malay Peninsula, just thirty miles north of the equator. It is surrounded by sea on three sides and a nearly impenetrable jungle to the north, and the British soldiers, expecting a naval attack from the Japanese, defended the south, east, and west sides of the garrison. When the Japanese crept through the jungle, they were able to take Singapore with little effort.

Fred Spencer escaped into the jungle, where he lived for nine months before he was finally reunited with his fellow British soldiers.

Before entering the jungle Spencer had heard two conflicting stories about what it would be like there. On the one hand he heard that it was a lush tropical paradise; that there were animals running around he could kill and eat, and trees and bushes that bowed down with berries and fruits to eat. According to this view, he should not have much trouble existing in quite grand style.

On the other hand, he had also heard the jungle was a harsh, impenetrable forest of creeping vines; that all of the fruits and berries were poisoned, the water was bad, and that he would die very quickly.

What he discovered was that neither was true. His experience taught him the "the jungle is neutral." He found that the jungle was neither out to destroy him nor support him. In actual fact he could survive in direct relationship to the effort he put forth to survive.

The important parallel here is that in the jungle called life, other than your belief in God, there is no great, mysterious force that is supportive or destructive. Life is neutral. The hand of fate will make no attempt to lift you up, nor will it hold you down.

Sociologists have actually studied this so-called "hand of fate" and have confirmed this. They have found that for one percent of the population, incredible bad luck does seem to be the rule. Their family is killed in a crime spree the same day they lose their jobs and the stock market crashes. For another one percent, the opposite holds true: They buy a ticket in the Irish Sweepstakes and overnight find themselves wealthy, or a rich, previously unheard of uncle dies, leaving them a fortune. But for the other ninety-eight percent of the population—you, me, and Fred Spencer—the success they have in their lives is in exact proportion to the effort they put forth.

CHAPTER 9
Personality Styles

If each of us is to get what he wants out of life, it is important for us to recognize that we each have a distinct personality style and that every person with whom we will be dealing also has a distinct personality style. Understanding this simple fact, and knowing how to change the way we do things in order to adapt to other personality styles, can make any negotiation go better for all parties concerned. Learning to get along with other personality styles in a negotiation can help you to feel more comfortable in any situation by understanding the other negotiators better—in a business situation, it can make all the difference.

I first became aware of differences in personality styles when I attended a "success rally" held at Anaheim Stadium in California. If you have never attended a success rally, let me explain that it can be a wild experience. A promoter will hire a giant stadium that can seat anywhere from 25,000 to 50,000 people. He'll bring in speakers from all over the country, speakers who usually have a positive message concerning success motivation.

While the message of each speaker may be similar, the styles of presentation are vastly different. When I was driving home with four of my friends who had also attended the rally, none of us could agree on who had been the best speaker. One of my friends said, "I loved the motivational speaker, the one who raced up and down the aisles and yelled and screamed, and had all those props up on stage. I loved the way he jumped up on the table and had the whole audience chanting together. He excited me! I really felt good about him and his presentation!"

Another said, "You know, I hate that kind of yelling and screaming. Why does a speaker have to yell at you? Why can't he just talk to you? I'm not a child; I went to the rally to find out something new, not to be entertained. That other speaker was much better in my opinion. He seemed to be very open and friendly, very nice. Sure, he owned a Rolls Royce, but I got the feeling that he'd lend it to me in a minute, if I asked him. I felt very comfortable with him, and as I looked around at the audience, I could see that everyone else was enjoying his speech too. He's the kind of person I would feel comfortable going up to after the rally and talking to. I would want to meet him again because I didn't feel overpowered."

Another of my friends said, "Well, I liked the speaker that you would probably say gave the worst presentation of all. He wasn't particularly dynamic—he had to refer to his notes quite a lot, but you have to admit that he gave us much more information in that short period of time than anybody else. That's all I really care about. I don't care about how much the speaker jumps up and down or how long he stands still—but he has to tell me something. Without information, why talk at all?"

The fourth, who happened to be an engineer, frowned and said, "I didn't care for the whole thing. I thought it was all too phony. I didn't like the hoopla and I didn't like the motivational music in between the speakers and I didn't like how all the presentations were hyped up. There weren't any handouts to give us the details of what a speaker was talking about, so we could follow along and analyze his presentation. We didn't get enough of an introduction on any of the speakers in terms of his academic credentials or where he got his information. How do they expect us to be able to analyze what they're saying? They don't tell us half of what we need to know."

It occurred to me that if a speaker can stand up in front of an audience and get four totally different responses, it follows that the same thing can happen when we are dealing face to face with people. A tactic that may be extremely effective in helping us to get what we want out of one type of person, may actually be antagonistic to our cause when we are dealing with someone else with a different kind of personality style. For this reason, it is obviously important that we learn to deal with the many styles of

167

personality that exist.

The first step is to study ourselves. Not until we know what our own personality style is, and its relationship with other styles, can we learn how to adapt that style in dealing with others. In order to do this we'll go through each of the four personality styles and work to identify your own personality. Try to select a style that most accurately describes you and your reactions to situations. You may see yourself in more than one category, perhaps one other, in which case you have a major style and a minor style, but it is impossible for you to feel comfortable in three or more of them. If you see yourself in each of the categories, you probably have real problems. So try to find one that fits you, or at the most, two.

The easiest way that I've found to help you identify your own style is to suggest a situation. Imagine that you have just come out of a three-hour seminar and are now in the coffee shop of the office building. You are waiting for the next seminar to start, and talking about the seminar you've just been to.

If you had the first personality style we're going to discuss, the pragmatic style, you would probably say something like this: "That was a pretty good seminar. We got a few very interesting ideas out of that. But did it really have to last for three hours? I bet if the speaker had taken all the stories and the jokes out of his presentation, he could have given us the same amount of information in half the time. And now that I think about it, they could have just mimeographed the highlights of the seminar and mailed it to us and we wouldn't have needed to come at all."

The pragmatic is a bottom-line person. He does not go to a seminar to be entertained. He wants to get straight to the point: the facts. The faster he can get those facts, with the less inconvenience, the better off he feels. The pragmatic is very conscious of time management. He's the type of person that is always phoning his office to see if there have been any messages for him. A pragmatic is an active person. For him to sit and watch anybody do anything is very difficult, especially if the action seems to have no tangible point. The pragmatic is a doer, not a watcher or a listener.

The second style is the extrovert. The extrovert will say about the seminar, "Wasn't that great! I really felt good. That guy was such a dynamic motivational speaker. He was one of the best I've ever seen. After listening to his message, I feel I can begin to take on a tough problem and solve it. And

168

wasn't the humor great? I wrote down all the jokes and can't wait until I get back to the office tomorrow so I can try them out."

The extrovert is a very emotional, easily motivated type of person. He is generally friendly, and easily impressed. The extrovert gets very excited about big projects, sometimes without thinking them out completely. His willingness to take risks, however, can often play in his favor. The extrovert is not deeply analytical, but he does have a good sense for the ins and outs of business.

The amiable is the third style of personality. This type of person is most likely to say of the seminar something like: "Wasn't the speaker a nice person? I got such a warm feeling when he was telling us about his family and his children. And I noticed that most of the other people in the room were enjoying his presentation just as much as I was. I liked the fact that he didn't tell any of those jokes that put down mothers-in-law or gay jokes or anything like that, because I do get offended very, very easily with that sort of thing. I felt good about the speaker, and I really enjoyed it."

The amiable person may not be able to tell you too much about the seminar's highlights a week after the seminar is over, but he will be able to tell you that he had a good time. The ambience in the room is very important to an amiable person, who loves people. He is also less analytical than an extrovert, and sometimes can get into trouble because of that trait. However, amiables tend to have an uncanny sense for where trouble lies, so most of the time they are able to steer clear of disaster.

The fourth type of personality, the analytical type, would think about the seminar for a moment and then say, "There were some good points, but they needed a lot more back-up. I mean, that speaker did in three hours what really should have taken at least five days, or maybe a ten-day symposium to go into it with any depth at all. We weren't able to look at—let alone discuss—any graphs or charts or statistics. I wish he'd gone into more detail; I think I also need to know a lot more about that speaker's academic background and professional experience before I can judge what he has to say. Without that, I can't really evaluate his presentation."

As you can see, an analytical person analyzes. He looks for the roots of a problem, and in many ways he's very different from the pragmatic. While a pragmatic person looks at the results, the analytical person seeks the causes. He wants to know every possible piece of information that could have a bearing on a problem before he starts to solve it. He is a thorough person, and while he may be slow in reaching his decisions, the conclusions he reaches generally hold up under even the closest scrutiny.

Take a look at the personality chart on the next page. As you can see, it's divided into four quadrants. Notice how each of the personality styles we've looked at fits into this system of quadrants. In the top righthand corner, you see the pragmatic; in the bottom righthand corner, the extrovert; in the bottom lefthand corner, the amiable; in the top lefthand quadrant, the analytical.

The horizontal line on this chart represents the level of assertiveness, with a high level of assertiveness being shown on the right, low on the left. When I say that pragmatics and extroverts have a high level of assertiveness, I mean that both of these types are take-charge people, always wanting to control things. Their attitude is: "If anyone is going to be running this thing, I'd rather it was me." If you're ever involved in a carpool, you'll see the validity of this. The pragmatic and the extrovert in the group will volunteer to drive, even if they have to pay for the gas. They would rather pay than relinquish control of the situation.

Over on the lefthand, low-assurance-level side, the attitude of amiables and analyticals is: "Fine, if you want to go ahead and be on the committee, that's okay with me. I've got other things to do that interest me more."

The vertical line illustrates the organizational level of the different personalities. At the top, the analyticals and pragmatics are fairly organized people. They have a very good sense for managing time and getting things done. They will have an organized work space and organized homes. Everything in their lives will be neat and tidy and in its place.

On the bottom side of the organizational level we find the extroverts and the amiables. These people tend to live in a more unstructured environment. They make decisions as problems present themselves, rather than well in advance, as do the pragmatics and analyticals. They plan very few of their activities—they're very spontaneous. Their work places are not tidy; in fact, they tend to be cluttered. These are the people who take true delight in disorder. They like to have their surroundings look lived-in.

Another way of looking at this vertical line might be as defining the emotional level of the different types, with the low level being on top. Using very little emotion, analyticals and pragmatics tend to make their decisions

"You'll always have the most difficulty with the personality diagonally opposite you on the chart."

based on cold, hard facts. Amiables and extroverts will look to their feelings as they make their choices.

To this chart I would like to add one more factor. On the righthand side, the pragmatics and extroverts have a very short attention span. Both personality styles have a very hard time sitting through a three-hour meeting or even a movie. There are always other things they want to do—things they feel should be done *right now*. Pragmatics and extroverts have their lives to live and are very uncomfortable when they have to just sit and watch. People with short attention spans tend to be faster decision makers. They will take a look at a proposition and either say yes or no fairly quickly. They don't want to take a lot of time to think it over. This is a very common attribute in assertive people.

Over on the lefthand side of the chart we find people with longer attention spans—the amiables and analyticals. These two personality types have much more patience than the other two. An analytical can sit through a ten-day symposium on the expansion of oxygen on the planet Mars in the year 2015 and walk away saying they haven't even scratched the surface of the topic. An amiable typically feels very, very close to people he hasn't seen at all for maybe ten years—his relationships last. These people have very long attention spans, and so their decision-making process takes an extremely long time. It is not unusual for an analytical person to take one or even two weeks thinking out a proposition before he finally decides. An amiable may not think a question out quite as thoroughly, but he will still take as much time as possible to make a final decision.

Here we find the first point of conflict in interpersonal relationships. If you are a pragmatic or an extrovert—in other words, a fast decision maker—and you're trying to deal with an amiable or an analytical, their slow decisions will drive you right up the wall! You can present a proposal to them and a week later they'll tell you they're still thinking about it. In that case, a pragmatic or an extrovert thinks, For heaven's sake, how long does it take this person to make up his mind? It's not natural for somebody to take that much time—there must be something wrong with him.

On the other hand, if you're an amiable or an analytical, you'll be very suspicious of the fast decisions that pragmatics and extroverts come to, and pressure you to make as well. You might spend a month or two preparing a proposal for your pragmatic boss to look at, and as you give it to him, you say, "I'll probably need to leave this with you for a few days so that you can look it over."

Your boss answers, "No, no, that's not necessary, let's take a look and make a decision right now." He'll glance quickly through your forty or fifty page proposal , ask you a couple of questions, then say, "I love it, let's do it." And you're very suspicious.

You are thinking, Oh, sure, he says he'll do it now, but what happens when something goes wrong and I need his support, will he be there backing me up? Does he really believe in this project strongly or is he just giving it lip service to get me off his back?

Slow decision makers are suspicious of the fast decision makers, and fast decision makers are irritated by the slow decision makers. This information can be quite helpful the next time you present a proposal to someone and he says, "I want to think it over." Before entering this situation, you should have tried to analyze the personality style of the person with whom you're dealing. When he tells you he wants to think over your proposal, and you know he's a pragmatic or an extrovert type—in other words, highly assertive— you might as well go ahead and press your point right there. You should push home your arguments now because you can be sure he'll be making *his* decision within the next few hours and next week may be too late to change his mind.

However, if you know you're dealing with a person who is not highly assertive, an amiable or analytical person, you should be aware that he probably *does* want more time to think it over. If you pressure him at this point, he may begin to wonder why you want an immediate decision—what's wrong with your proposal that will become apparent if he has a chance to look through it? He'll be very suspicious and therefore very cautious.

As you can see, each personality style can encounter quite a few problems when dealing with others. These conflicts may be avoided or at least ameliorated, however, once we know not only what style we ourselves are, but what style the other person in the negotiation is. For this reason, now that you've had a chance to analyze yourself, let's talk more about each personality, so you can begin to analyze the people around you and better understand how to deal with them effectively.

The Pragmatic

The pragmatic surrounds himself with time-efficiency gadgets. I don't mean that he's a gadget hound—someone who owns gadgets because he loves little things that squeak and move around and are entertaining—no, the pragmatic wants a gadget to help him save time, and anything that will give him a few more minutes in his day, he wants. A pragmatic will be the first person in town to have an answering machine. You remember when those things first appeared on the market, everyone was saying, "Isn't that awful? Now they expect us to talk to machines!" Everyone, that is, except the pragmatic, who bought one the first day it was in the store. It never even occurred to him that someone else might think it was cold and impersonal.

A pragmatic will run a very efficient office, in terms of environment. He will have a hard time working amidst clutter. He'll certainly have a secretary who screens his calls before she tells him there's someone on the line, and places his telephone calls for him, an often irritating experience for the person being called: "Mr. Dawson, Mr. Smith is holding for you. He's on the line, would you hold for just a moment, please?" It can be especially infuriating when there are two pragmatics dealing with each other and both secretaries have been instructed not to put their boss on the line until the other person is on it!

The pragmatic's work space will be very organized. He probably will not come out into the lobby to greet you when you arrive to see him. He'll have his secretary come out. If there is any delay at all, the secretary will say, "Mr. Dawson, I'm sorry, but Mr. Smith is running a little late today. It will probably be another five minutes before he'll be able to see you. If you don't mind being patient, I'll come in and get you just as soon as he's ready." And then she'll usher you quickly into the office.

The pragmatic is *very* conscious of the passage of time. His whole day is organized and broken down into five-minute increments. He hates the thought of wasting any of his day. For example, he enjoys watching the national news on television because that way he'll get a capsulized digest of everything that's happened during the day. If the news is supposed to come on at seven P.M. and he enters the living room and finds it's only 6:58, he'll be very annoyed. "Darn it!" he might say to himself. "I'm two minutes early— what in the world am I going to do for two minutes?" So he'll pick up a book and read it for two minutes. After the news comes on he'll finish an extra half page during the commercials. When the news is winding down to the last oddball human interest story of the day, the pragmatic will turn it off because he is just not interested in that sort of inconsequential entertainment.

If you happen to be married to a pragmatic, you know that when they go on vacation, they like to *go*. A pragmatic finishes work at five-thirty in the evening, and chances are he'll have booked a flight that leaves at six-thirty, giving him just enough time to go home, pack, and leave for the airport.

The best example of a pragmatic that I have ever seen was Dolly Parton's boss in the movie *Nine to Five*. You remember, the guy who kept chasing her around the office (*that* is not necessarily a trait of pragmatics!). The last thing he wanted to do was go on vacation but his wife kept bringing him brochures and travel guides to try and persuade him to decide on a trip. Finally, he took time out of his schedule to listen to her proposals, but when he learned she was talking about a two-week cruise through the Caribbean, he said, "Wait a minute, do I have this straight? You want me to spend two weeks of my life floating around on some tuna boat?"

The thought of doing nothing haunts pragmatics. They have nightmares about being idle. For that reason, pragmatics do not generally like spectator sports. The idea of going down to a stadium and watching someone else do something for three or four hours is just beyond their tolerance. If they like sports, they like to be involved, doing something: fishing, hunting, team sports, or sports like tennis or golf, where they can play.

For a pragmatic the key words are *be involved*. A pragmatic will almost always be the driving force behind an enterprise. They like to be in charge, they like to do things, and usually delegate a great number of responsibilities simply because of time pressures—however, their slogan is, "don't expect unless you inspect." Pragmatics are hardworking, decisive, very efficient, and above all, active.

The Extrovert

The extrovert is also assertive. But while the pragmatic goes crazy if he isn't doing something, the extrovert likes nothing better than spec-

"The pragmatic surrounds himself with time efficiency gadgets."

tator sports. For an extrovert to be down at the stadium, sharing in the emotion of a great crowd, is just about as good as life can get. It's heaven.

The extrovert is first and foremost a very friendly, open person. He places his own telephone calls. The extrovert most certainly will *not* have his calls screened. He'll pick up the phone in his office and say, "Roger, this is Joe. What can I do for you today?" A caller may go through a secretary but the secretary won't ask who's calling or stumble around the question of whether or not the boss is in. A secretary may answer the call, but the call will go right through if the boss is in; and if the secretary isn't there to answer the phone, then the extrovert will just pick it up himself and go right on.

If a visitor comes to meet the extrovert, he'll will probably meet him in the lobby of the building, give the visitor a tour, and say "Hi" to everyone who works there as he walks around.

The extrovert will have pictures of his family in the office, whereas the pragmatic would tend to think that pictures of the kids are a little too informal for a business atmosphere. The extrovert will talk to you in a friendly way, even when you move on to such non-business subjects as vacation, sports, or the weather, but if the extrovert is interrupted by someone, he'll give a quick businesslike decision.

The extrovert makes up his mind quickly and is not afraid to say no to people, although he always tries to do it in a friendly way. He's the type of person who can step on your toes without messing up the shine on your shoes.

He is not, however, a very organized person. His desk tends to be filled with *stuff*, for example, and the extrovert is not very good at following up on things. He tends to leave a wake of unfinished projects behind him.

The extrovert is excited, decisive, and he'll jump very quickly at a new project. He'll get that project going and everyone will be thrilled with it, but when it reaches to the follow-through stage, or the picky-detail steps, the extrovert becomes very weak.

The extrovert makes decisions very quickly, but is quite emotional. He'll see something and want it. Real estate agents know how to pull out the "curb appeal" properties for this type of buyer. By curb appeal, I mean the way a property looks from the street, when a buyer first sees it. If a house looks like Tara from *Gone With the Wind*, with big white columns out in front, chances are the extrovert buyer will be sold on it before he even walks in

177

"The extrovert loves spectator sports."

the door. He'll love it and want it, and all the agent has to do is go along.

Extroverts tend to pick their spouses that way too. An extrovert will walk into a cocktail party, and standing at the bar will the next great love of his life. Within minutes his decision has been made.

Extroverts are fantastic starters but not very good finishers. They have a sense of humor and like to be part of a crowd. They're very assertive and can be very businesslike while maintaining an atmosphere of warmth and informality. Extroverts can accomplish a great deal, and at the same time make friends.

The Amiable

Amiables tend to build barriers around themselves. An amiable has an unlisted telephone number, and his is the house with the No Peddlers sign over the doorbell. An amiable will stay in one neighborhood for a long, long time, because amiables form lasting bonds of affection with people and surroundings. An amiable will like the home in which he lives and like the furniture and the color of the walls because he's attached to it.

Amiables tend to drive older cars than most, because they can't bear to sell an old friend. The last thing in the world that an amiable would want to do is to buy a new car, because he knows that when he gets to the lot he'll be pressured by the salesman about trading in his old, familiar car and about how much he's willing to pay for a new one. An amiable is easily ground down under high pressure.

Amiables are very seldom found in positions of higher management, because of their incapacity to deal with stress. The only time you'll find an amiable in an upper level is in a large corporation, where he can exist fairly well because of the structured environment. In a large corporation, he can be assertive (even though he's naturally not very assertive) by requiring his subordinates to follow his instructions (rather than his having to do unpleasant things that might displease his co-workers). An amiable type dislikes having to play the role of bad guy, and so he's very easily taken advantage of, unless his position is secure.

An amiable tends to be disorganized, but surprisingly enough, extroverts do not generally approve of or like amiables. Unlike extroverts, who main-

"Amiables form lasting bonds of affection with people and surroundings."

tain a businesslike attitude, amiables have no sense of time management at all. If someone telephones an amiable and says, "When can I come over to see you?" more likely than not, the answer will be, "Oh, just drop by any time." An extrovert would be more decisive: "Why don't you come over at noon on Friday? Then we can have a bite to eat and discuss things." A pragmatic, on the other hand, would say something like, "First, could I ask you what this is all about? Are you sure it's not something we can just settle over the phone?"

Amiables tend to get disorganized—even more than normal—because they find it difficult to say no to people. Whenever they're asked to be on a committee or a board of directors, or in charge of this or that, they lack the assertiveness to say, "No, I just can't right now. I've got too much going on and I just couldn't handle any more responsibilities. Thanks for the offer, but please ask somebody else." Therefore, they tend to take on more than they can handle, and often end up not doing any of it well.

Amiables are very warm, nice people. They tend to develop deep attachments to people and things, and have the capacity to remember a face in a crowd, your first name, and the age of your oldest child. Amiables are very good at spotting the moods of a crowd, since they're extremely sensitive. They're also observant and generally quite knowledgeable. If they have a fault, it's being too weak when it comes to putting their feet down or exerting pressure when necessary. They just like people too much to do anything that might jeopardize their reputation for being good-hearted.

The Analytical

The analytical person is most likely to be identified by his profession, and will often be an engineer or an accountant because he loves detailed work with lots of picky things involved in it. He has the gadget mania. He's the person who owns the combination wood-burning stove/garden hose/pasta maker. He enjoys the little moving squeaking things with small details, and is the one with pens in his pocket that have built-in calculators or clocks.

You used to be able to spot an analytical just from the slide rule in his

181

"It used to be just the slide rule in the pocket that identified the Analytical."

pocket, but now the thing to watch for is the fancy watch that tells the weather and the latest stock market figures as well as the time, and doubles as a television set. Pretty soon it will be a battery-operated Apple computer they can carry around with them.

An analytical is very curious. Show an analytical a book and he'll want to know how it's bound and where it's distributed. An analytical practically soaks up information; he'll soak up tremendous amounts of data, even if the information is from a field that doesn't particularly interest him.

Analytical people don't like to shoot from the hip with an answer. They like to think about all sides of a question before they commit themselves to voicing a solution. They're very slow to make a decision but the decisions they do make are very well considered and usually take into account the most far-reaching circumstances.

Because analyticals are so slow, many are prone to be pipe smokers. Ask an analytical what day of the week it is and he'll want to think about the implications of the question before he'll tell you it's Wednesday. So, while he thinks, he'll suck on his pipe, maybe poke in it a little, and relight it with one of those lighters that looks like a flame thrower—the kind that works upside down. Finally, after a great deal of thought and concentration, he'll say, "It's Wednesday. . . in most parts of the world."

An analytical is fascinated by—you guessed it—analysis. He will have a chart or a graph for everything. I once knew a man who was in charge of a very large corporation and he virtually ran his business with charts, thousands upon thousands of charts; he had charts covering every facet of his business, from a list of every single person working for him to the number of staples each office had in stock. Everything had to be on a chart or a graph, and then analyzed, with dots and lines in all colors going off in every direction.

The analytical's theory of management is not inspirational, as is that of the extrovert, but rather his philosophy is founded in the firm belief that if each person analyzes where he is at any given moment and then analyzes where he wants to go, it will be a lot easier to end up there. He also believes that such analysis leads people to automatically strive harder to reach their goals. There's a great deal to be said for that philosophy. . . at least, it seems to work well for the analyticals.

The problem with that theory, and with many analyticals, however, is

183

that most of them seem to spend most of their time filling out charts and graphs and figuring out the problems, and very little time actually *doing* anything.

Analyticals are very punctual. When an analytical says he'd like to see you at 10:05, he means *exactly* 10:05, and not 10:05 and fifteen seconds. They are very precise about punctuality, very precise about figures. If an analytical asks you how much something costs, never say, "Oh, I think it's somewhere around a hundred dollars." It would be far better to say to him, "Let me check it out and get back to you. I'll have the figure for you sometime tomorrow," and the next day call him up and say, "It will be $104.67." The answer of about a hundred dollars would be just fine for an extrovert, but an analytical will be severely unimpressed by your obvious lack of information if you're that vague. He would much rather have you offer to find out than have you tell him something imprecise.

Analyticals are scientific types — lovers of firm, concrete facts. They enjoy learning and analyzing ever more information. They're slow decision makers but they are not afraid to say no, and usually their decisions will be good enough to hold up even under the most difficult of situations. An analytical is generally very withdrawn — more interested in gadgets and details than relationships — but the friends he does have will be good friends, people who have known him most of his life.

As we look at these four personality styles, I want you to be aware that you'll always have the most trouble dealing with the style exactly opposite yours on the chart. For example, if you're a pragmatic, you'll have the most trouble dealing with an amiable. If you're an extrovert, you will find it very difficult to deal with an analytical, and vice versa.

I've given you enough information about personality styles to be able to identify not only your own style, but the differing styles of personality you deal with every day. Take a minute right now and analyze a few of the people you come in contact with daily. Take any single co-worker or friend and try to determine which of the four personality types that person fits into. Of course, almost nobody will fit into one category without having any of the attributes of the other categories. But it's surprising how easy it is to identify the dominant characteristics of almost every person you know.

I've spent quite a bit of time on this subject because I feel that it's one of the most important factors in not only negotiating successfully, but in working with other people every day—in every way. Think of that one person in the office you really can't stand to work with . . . the one who drives you crazy. Chances are that person is exactly the opposite personality from you and it's the diametrically opposing personality styles that are the source of the clash.

By taking the time to analyze another person's personality style, you'll find it much easier to communicate with him. If you are an amiable and you're faced with an obvious pragmatic, go to extra lengths to be more highly structured. Ignore your instinct to spend time breaking the ice with small talk. Be prepared with facts and figures, and get to the bottom line quickly. If, on the other hand, you're the pragmatic dealing with an amiable, try to take a little more time and put the other person at ease. Ask about his or her family; steer the negotiation to a conclusion, but have patience.

The extra effort spent analyzing and adjusting to different personality styles will pay for itself many times over in the form of goodwill, and you'll find that your new-found understanding of other people will allow you to get much more out of life.

SUCCESS COMMENTARY

Learning to Love Change

Ever since Alvin Toffler wrote the book *Future Shock*, people have been running around horrified at the supposedly monumental changes taking place in our society, and wondering whether human beings can withstand such change.

It's an interesting concept, but I'm really not sure it's that applicable. When you think about it, the changes he describes are rather superficial. Substantial changes, the kind that change the way men think, have been few and far between.

In fact, I would go so far as to say that since the start of civilization there have only been four people who haved caused Western man to change the way he thinks of his world.

The first was Jesus Christ. Until he started to preach, we didn't realize that there was a life force we could tap into. Regardless of your religious persuasion, his ministry was a remarkable turning point for mankind.

The second was Galileo. It wasn't until Galileo publicized his belief in Copernicus' theory of the solar system that we realized the earth is not the center of the universe.

The third person was Charles Darwin. Until he promoted his theory of evolution, we were totally convinced that we were a divine creation of God. Darwin raised the frightening possibility that we might just be a biological accident.

And the fourth person was Sigmund Freud. Until he revealed to us the secrets of the subconscious mind, we thought we were in total control of our thoughts.

We shouldn't be so concerned about the minor changes that Alvin Toffler talks about. Man is a creature of change—the only creature of change, in fact. Put a horse into a field and it will always be a field. Put a man into a field and there's no telling what he might make of it.

To become more adaptable to change, start with the little things. If you've made a habit of always driving to work the same way, of going to lunch with the same people and always ordering the same cocktail—make a conscious effort to vary your routine. It will make you more observant and more aware of your surroundings. And who knows—maybe you'll get to like change so much that I'll run into you one day sailing to Tahiti or climbing in the Himalayas.

CHAPTER 10
Negotiating Styles

In this chapter we are going to discuss the relationship between a person's personality style and the negotiating style he subsequently develops. As a negotiator you'll find that the more you understand the personality styles of the people around you, both your co-workers and the people that you are negotiating with, the easier your job will be.

As a negotiator, the pragmatic tends to turn into a *street fighter.* A street fighter is someone going through the negotiating process in order to get what he wants. A pragmatic has his goals clearly before him, and with his mania for efficiency, is going to fight hard to get what he wants quickly. His attitude is, "I don't quite understand this idea of win-win negotiating. Don't expect me to look out for the goals of the other people in this negotiation. That's what they're here for. I'm here to fight as hard as I can for what I want, and I expect them to fight just as hard."

The pragmatic pulls no punches; he fights hard and low, and for him, there are very few justifications for giving in and making concessions during a negotiation. He is out to get what he wants—and that's all.

The extrovert, on the other hand, tends to turn into a *den mother* when put into a negotiating situation. A den mother is someone who's so enthusiastic about the project he's involved in that he seems to lose sight of the fact that he's dealing with other people who aren't necessarily as enthusiastic as he is.

This is the person in your office who is trying to organize an employee

189

softball team, and it never occurs to him for a moment that there are people in your office who don't think a good game of softball is the perfect way to spend every Tuesday night. The extrovert thinks it's just a matter of getting everyone else as excited as he is, a task often doomed from the start.

The amiable, the exact opposite of the street-fighting pragmatic, turns into a *pacifier* during the negotiations. His goals are not to win in the negotiations, as are the street fighter's, but to create and maintain an atmosphere in which everyone involved is happy.

If he can keep the other negotiators happy, the amiable feels he's succeeded in negotiating, no matter how many concessions he has to make or how conciliatory his attitude has to remain. All he wants is to find a solution agreeable to everyone, even if it doesn't meet the requirements he would have wished.

The analytical negotiator is by nature an *executive*. An executive is someone who lives in such a rigid world that any attempt to get him to be flexible will be met with intransigence. To the analytical any sign that he's not absolutely set in his course—because he has studied the facts and he *knows*—will be viewed as a sign of weakness. The analytical's favorite expression is, "It's the principle of the thing."

For the extrovert, who is the opposite of the analytical-executive in personality style, this is a particularly difficult situation. The extrovert will find himself saying, "Look, we're only talking about five hundred dollars here. Let's just split the difference and get this deal moving."

The executive will answer, "I understand perfectly that we're only talking about a five hundred dollar spread here, and that does seem a bit silly. But, since your suggestion to split the difference demonstrates your willingess to come down, that means that we're only discussing a spread of two hundred and fifty dollars. The point is, it's the principle of the thing at this stage."

The analytical is generally positive that he has studied every aspect of the possible agreement and that his conclusions are the only possible conclusions, given the circumstances. Therefore, any attempt by the other side to give, hoping that he'll give as well, will only prove to him that the other side hasn't studied all the facts. If their case were as good as his, he thinks, they would not be so quick to give in.

If you are an analytical type, the first advice I would give you is to reexamine your position during a negotiation. Are you being too inflexible in

190

"The Pragmatic tends to turn into a street fighter."

your demands? If you are, it may be time to learn to give part of the way.

Now we want to compare all of these different styles in an actual negotiating situation. Let's say that four investors have gotten together and have each contributed $250,000 so that together they have one million dollars. With this starting capital the four hope to go into business together and begin manufacturing widgets. The ultimate goal of this team is to eventually dominate the world market in widget manufacture.

As they meet for the first planning session, to work out how the company should be organized, how it will run, and where it will be built, it becomes clear that each member of the team is entering the negotiation with a different personality style. In this group we have a street fighter, a den mother, a pacifier, and an executive. This could be the beginning of a long, drawn-out battle for power.

Fortunately, in this case, the four parties concerned have taken some of their starting capital and hired a needs negotiator — a neutral third party to act as an arbitrator in case of an impasse. This person can sit in with them while they negotiate and act as an expert in the decisions concerning how the company will be formed.

In the first stage of negotiation each of the parties should learn the objectives of the others. This is where the goals of each person are presented. In this case, we will note not only what the goals of each of these personality styles are, but also how each person presents these goals: how each member of the team presents his point of view and the objectives as he sees them.

The first thing anyone will present is his goal. If we start with the street fighter, we see that his goal is nothing more or less than victory. He has a particular view of the way things should be run and wants to impress upon the other members of the team that he's right, and is going to enter the negotiations swinging, and will fight to win — regardless of whatever anyone else thinks. In the opinion of the street fighter personality, the only purpose for having a discussion at all is for each party to express his views and try to *win*.

His attitude is, What's all this nonsense about giving in to the other guy? Why should I be expected to look out for the needs of everyone else during a negotiation? We're all adults here — we aren't here to get to know each other

"Den Mothers (Extroverts) blind themselves to reality."

better or to be entertained. We're here to get what we want. And if it's a question of what I want or what he wants, I'll pick what I want every time.

The street fighter is going to fight hard and fast for as long as he can in order to get what he wants, otherwise he feels he's wasted his time.

The den mother has the extrovert's desire to influence as his goal. He doesn't particularly care which side of the controversy he takes, in fact he'll take any position available as long as he can influence other people.

The extrovert feeds on emotion and likes to create that emotion in other people and build it up to a level that can match his. He wants everyone else to be as excited as he is. Therefore, his main goal is to be able to control the rest of the group with his powers of influence.

His tactics will be rather sneaky. Very often, he will just sit and listen to the other three members of the group to learn their objectives in order to be sure that when he picks a position, it won't be the same position as someone else in the negotiations, because that would take most of the fun out of the game. The extrovert doesn't want to see how strongly he can support someone else's position, he wants to see how many people he can influence into supporting his own, no matter what that is.

The extrovert will wait through most of the first stage of a negotiation and then pick a position different from the other three. From then on his goal is to influence the others. That is the key word in his life — influence. Regardless of his position, and regardless of whether he is right or wrong, the extrovert's goal is to influence other people to accept his point of view.

The third personality style, the amiable, will adopt the attitude of peacemaker. His point of view would be expressed as: "I know we have to find an agreement here, and I know we will. I just want that agreement to be something everyone involved can really be happy with, and I want us to be able to be friends after the negotiation is over."

For the amiable type, finding the right objective for the group — discussing the best way to manufacture and distribute widgets — will always take a back seat to the goal of having all parties as pleased as possible with the outcome of the negotiation. Thus he is often willing to compromise on even the most important points, so as to maintain what he considers to be a friendly mood. He'll do his best to minimize pressure and stress within the meeting and most likely lose whatever position he does take, simply because he has no real desire to win.

The analytical personality style, the executive negotiator, has as his main objective in the meeting the desire for order. He wants the meeting to be set up in such a way that everyone involved is forced to work within a very rigid structure. He wants the minutes taken correctly. He wants the proper points of order to be followed. He is set on having the meeting run smoothly, if only because he won't allow anyone to speak out of turn.

The executive negotiator will also fight hard for what he wants, because he is convinced that what he wants is the only possible solution that can be reached through a logical study of the facts. He has a desire to win— and win on a certain set of points, unlike the extrovert, who just wants to win but doesn't really care what position he wins on.

Of course, the neutral negotiator observing this proceeding is seeing the entire situation from a very different standpoint. His objective is the most simple and in many ways also the most admirable—all the neutral negotiator wants out of the negotiations is a wise settlement for the group, without regard for which person wins or loses. The person whose position prevails and the person whose position does not prevail—these are not his concern. His concern is a wise set of decisions pertaining to the use of the investment capital.

As we move from the first stage of negotiations to the second, we must become aware of one of the most pivotal factors in any negotiation: the interrelations of the parties involved. How does each party deal with the others as they fight for their separate goals and negotiate for the use of one million dollars? The stakes are high, and as we look at the parties in this particular negotiation, it's interesting to note how much influence each personality style has, as every person is guided first by his personality, and only then by his concern for the wise management of the new business.

The street fighter tends to enter the negotiation swinging. He threatens and even if he doesn't come right out with his ultimatum, it is always implied: "Gentlemen, if you don't go along with what I say and what I want to do, then I'm going to get very angry. This could turn out to be an extremely unpleasant experience for all of us if that happens and you're not going to like it one little bit. So, if you want to avoid that sort of situation, I suggest you take my suggestions and go along with what I want to do."

The pragmatic (street fighter) will use the practical side of the negotiations to his benefit. He will emphasize that the negotiations will be a waste of time for *everyone*, not just him, if no solution can be reached. And if he's not given some of the points he considers important, then no settlement can be reached. It's as simple as that.

The extrovert personality, the den mother, begins by using his relationship with the parties involved to try and influence them to agree with him. He'll give motivational speeches in the committee meetings, call up everyone at home after hours, do his best to get everyone in the room as excited about his point of view as he is.

As he tries to enthuse everyone else in the negotiations, he may not realize that while his approach may have a great deal of effect over any other extroverts who happen to be in the room, his enthusiastic harangues have no such stimulating effect on the other personality styles present (and may even turn off the pragmatic).

His emotional approach does have a small amount of appeal for the amiable types in the meeting but they might feel pressured by his heavy emotionalism, and as amiables have little drive to win anyway, they tend to go wherever it seems they'll be achieving the most for *everyone*—which might rule out the extrovert's position from the first. Extroverts often use the emotion they can generate as a means of influencing members on a committee, as if he were a cheerleader at a football game. Unfortunately, while the extrovert's heart is undoubtedly in his effort, it usually doesn't work very well.

The pacifier sees his role as one of developing relationships. During the coffee breaks he will make a special point of getting together to chat with the other participants in the negotiations. He lets the other parties to the negotiation know how much he respects their position, in fact, how much he really agrees with their position and respects the fact that they're working so hard to achieve such valuable goals.

The amiable person tries to increase his ability to influence people by developing personal relationships with them. As this really is his strength, it's not a bad idea, especially if he's dealing with other amiables. But for the other three personality styles, the line between social and business relationships is quite strong, and they have very little difficulty in forming a friendship with a person on the opposing side during a coffee break and then going back to the negotiation to argue as before, their positions unchanged.

The goal of the executive negotiator is simply to ignore the different personalities involved and forge an agreement. The attitude of the analytical

"The Amiable turns into a pacifier."

personality dictates that what matters in business is not what kind of personalities his co-workers have but rather the structure of the dealings and the final decisions. The executive negotiator often does not understand that any negotiation will be affected by the personalities of the people involved. He sees meetings not as a place to develop relationships but as a place to develop solutions. He feels that if the negotiators can put a set of rules together and then develop the bylaws of a corporation in an efficient manner, it really won't matter what the individual personalities in the group think.

The neutral negotiator sits back in his chair and tries to separate the people from the problems. He has been a part of enough negotiations to be comfortable and familiar with all of the personalities represented in this negotiation. He knows what each personality style wants; he knows why each person operates the way he does and sees that to do his job he must wait and watch until he can see what the underlying concerns of the new corporation are, beneath all of the bluster of different personal goals.

The neutral negotiator must work to define, then probe, and finally solve the real problems of the corporation. His job is to be done without the influence of any of the personality styles—he must decide how best to invest one million dollars in the manufacture of widgets and at the same time to penetrate the widget market.

As we have seen, the style of the street fighter is to be hard and tough—to take a positive, incontrovertible stand. The den mother, the extrovert, is excitable. The amiable pacifier is very soft in the negotiations, not wanting to alienate anyone by giving strong opinions or fighting hard. And the executive is very detached from the people involved in the negotiations. In contrast, the neutral negotiator must be neither completely hard nor completely soft. He must be very soft on the personalities involved and very hard on the problems.

The negotiator has to be warm and friendly to all personality styles. He must never get angry or excited. He must be swayed by no one but, instead, practically present the problem in such a way that all personality styles must learn to deal with it: "Gentlemen, this is what we are trying to accomplish. What will lead us to the wisest investment for our money? The investment that will give us the deepest inroads into the widget market we're attempting to control?"

The negotiator must keep hammering at the problem, bringing it back

"The executive-style negotiator does everything by the rule book."

up into the discussion every time the subject changes to something more personality oriented. He must keep the group focused on the objectives they have as a group; soft on the people, very hard on the problem.

I probably don't have to mention that each of these personalities have faults, but I will. I want to point out the most basic fault in each of these personalities so that you can recognize the almost disastrous effects that these flaws can have on a negotiation.

The street fighter's most obvious negotiating flaw is his tendency to dig into a position and hold it until the last breath is drawn. He gets set on a very specific position, maybe something like, "We need to manufacture every part of our own widgets. It's not a good idea to farm them out." He will stick to that negotiating position because he is absolutely determined to win. He'll often be so determined, in fact, that even if a contrary opinion is presented — that widgets should be farmed out because it is much more economical — and the idea makes sense, he will still reject it to the point of losing in the negotiations. He would rather become a loser than give up what he perceives as a winning position.

With the extrovert personality, the den mother style tends to ignore the feelings of the other parties in a negotiation. An enthusiastic, excitable person can sometimes reach the point of being so enthusiastic and excited that he becomes blinded to the realities of the negotiation. He continues to pursue a point and try to get everyone else enthused about it even though nobody else is listening to him anymore. Remember, the extrovert is the one organizing a softball team at the office and is so excited about the project that it never occurs to him there is someone out there who doesn't want to play softball. Or he is the Scout leader who is so enthusiastic about taking all the Scouts up into the mountains for a picnic that he doesn't hear when some of the Scouts tell him they aren't interested in going on a picnic. The den mother becomes a loser because he tends not to notice when his position is passed by for a better one.

The fault of the pacifier is that he is too easily swayed. The amiable type is so intent on not causing friction between members of the group, wanting everyone to like him, that he will move from a position that he knows to be right. Because he feels that if the other parties in the negotiation don't like him he'll lose his ability to present his opinion, he often finds himself changing his opinions. The pacifier doesn't have the courage of his convictions. He cannot stand up and speak out for what he believes in. The pacifier tends to lose in the negotiations because he willingly gives his position away.

Inflexibility is the main fault of the executive negotiator. In the midst of his analytical personality style, the executive is often surrounded by rules and numbers and regulations and therefore tends to be rigid in his own feelings about the way things should be done. When the executive is asked for some kind of compromise in his position, he will often see it not as a way to a win-win negotiation, but as a sign of weakness. The whole time that he is negotiating, the executive is saying to himself, "If I could just get these other people to see that we need to structure this thing. All we need to do is structure—we need to build an organization and let the organization be the business for us. We really need to concentrate on the framework, and spell out clear goals for everyone, so that there is no deviation from those goals. We have to set up the levels of authority and clear up who reports to whom, so that everyone knows exactly what he can and can't do." The executive tends to feel like a loser if the agreement reached is not exactly what he wants, even though that agreement might be just as good or even better.

In summary, the street fighter (pragmatic) demands losses. He takes a position, and it is quite clear to him that there must be a winner and a loser in the negotiation and he's going to be the winner. The den mother (extrovert) demands excitement and acceptance. He tends to lose what supporters he has because, after the negotiations, they feel they were duped by motivational talk. With the den mother there is always the feeling that if you follow him, you're actually being swayed by a sales pitch.

The pacifier accepts losses too easily. He will present a position, but if it doesn't get immediate acceptance, he'll retreat from the position because he feels it's more important that the other parties like and respect him than they like and respect his position. The executive leans on rigidity, wanting clear courses of actions that are backed up statistically by charts and graphs.

The neutral negotiator must find a position that will be the best for everyone. He has the job of pointing up new options—solutions where no one has to feel as if he lost and where everyone can feel he's done his part to create a successful agreement. The negotiator works to make each party forget his personal positions and work for the common good.

The neutral negotiator must refute the street fighter's hold on a certain set of points. He recognizes that the street fighter's pragmatic nature has made a quick decision and is sticking to it because he does not want to waste his time rethinking his position. He must understand the pragmatic's personality and work to change his mind through logic.

He must face the den mother's excessive need for enthusiasm by understanding that when the extrovert is able to enthuse the others, they're not necessarily convinced, just motivated. It never occurs to the extrovert that there is not necessarily a connection between confidence and enthusiasm. If the extrovert sees someone who doesn't know what he's doing and then tries to enthuse that person into positive action, he does not realize that he may just persuade that person to keep on doing what he's doing, but with more speed and enthusiasm. When that happens, the other person is still doing something wrong, but with greater conviction, and that could be very harmful. The negotiator must persuade the extrovert to tone down his motivational rhetoric so that the other parties may reach their own conclusions in their own ways.

The negotiator then has to realize that for an amiable type who feels that his demands for a peaceful settlement are quite simple, the absence of a quiet, peaceful resolution at the end of the day will leave him feeling the meeting was not productive at all. The pacifier only wants one thing out of a meeting—total agreement. If that one thing is not accomplished, no matter how much is, he will feel like a loser. Therefore, the pacifier will often support a bad idea in the interests of an early settlement. The negotiator must show the pacifier that many things have been accomplished while encouraging him to promote his original good ideas.

As he faces an executive, the negotiator sees a person demanding a system. He feels that a system must be formed because people always work within systems. He thinks that people do not necessarily think for themselves or naturally develop initiative. He feels that his co-workers need to understand what a system is, learn what the organization should be, and then follow it. The negotiator must show the executive/analytical type that he is working with people with distinct, often powerful personalities—people who can think for themselves and whose ideas may seem just as right to them as his appear to him. The negotiator must show the executive that he *can* compromise without losing the negotiations.

The needs negotiator has only one demand—a solution. He understands very clearly what each of the personality styles wants to accomplish and works to enable each negotiator to abandon his personal interests in favor of the group. He knows that if he can convince each of the negotiators to stop fighting for their own private positions, they will be able to serve the mutual interests of the group.

We can see a fascinating example of this in the cold war going on right now. The United States is looking at the Soviet Union and saying, "Why do we even bother going through the farce of a negotiation with you? You are not going to change from your position. You are out to dominate the world and we've known that ever since Krushchev first pounded his shoe on the table at the United Nations. You won't quit until you have exported your revolution all over the world, until we are 'buried.' Why do we even bother to talk to you?"

No doubt, on the other side of the world, they're looking back at the United States and saying, "You Americans are capitalists. You are intent on *selling* your philosophy around the world, and we don't want to pay for it. You have social problems but you won't admit them, you just want us to change. You aren't open to our point of view, you reject our system without hearing our side. You pretend you're listening, but it's just a game. Why should we waste our time trying to talk to you?"

You can see the positions each side is taking. Their positions are at opposite ends of the spectrum and neither of them is willing to give, and yet, their interests are exactly the same. Both want world peace. Neither wants a nuclear holocaust. Both want freedom and security. Neither wants war.

Just as in the cold war, the neutral negotiator's task is to help each party forget his position and remember his interests. Personality styles determine positions, but good common sense can make each party aware of his interests. By emphasizing the goals of the *group*, the negotiator who is trying to help the four personality styles form a widget manufacturing company can keep on arguing and working until he has guided the negotiators to the best investment of their one million dollars in the widget market.

In your own negotiating situations I want to encourage you to work in the same way as the neutral negotiator. First, you must recognize your natural negotiating style—the one determined by your personality—and learn to overcome its faults. You must then learn to understand the other negotiating styles, and finally try to lead each style away from its natural position to the common interests of the group. Once you have become comfortable with this procedure, your negotiations will easily reach a win-win solution rather than one in which each personality style feels like a loser.

SUCCESS COMMENTARY

From Panic to Self-Actualization

If, in the delivery room at the hospital, some prophet magically confronted us with all of the problems we'd have to face in life, we'd all want to climb right back into the womb. But taken one day at a time, life becomes an exciting adventure.

I'm sure we've all had mornings when the sheer immensity of the problems we must face in the days ahead makes us want to pull the covers back over our heads. That feeling is called panophobia—the fear of everything.

Psychologists tell us there are basically six states of mind. The very lowest level is panic—when things are so bad that we blindly strike out. A widow at a funeral frequently has to fight off feelings of panic. The next stage up is inertia—the Monday morning feeling when we lose the battle of mind over mattress. Beyond that we find striving—when we know we have to start accomplishing things in life but can't conjure up the motivation. Then coping—getting by but not accomplishing very much. As we progress beyond this stage we finally have our act together and are living our lives for nothing but the sheer joy of fulfillment—we call it self-actualization, a term coined by Abraham Maslow.

A fully self-actualizing person is a joy to be around—that's the person who just took off to paint in Connecticut, completely free of any desire to impress anybody or change their life-style in order to gain friends; or the man putting the finishing touches on the boat he's going to sail to Tahiti.

We should all have two days when we completely divorce ourselves from our problems, and those two days should be yesterday and tomorrow. As a philosopher once pointed out, it isn't today that drives men mad but the regret over the past and fear of the future.

How, then, can we avoid those moments of our life spent in between panic and inertia? Of course we'd panic if we had to try and comprehend all of life's problems at one time. So we live through troubled times one day at a time. But the people who keep functioning through the toughest of times are those who have a strong sense of time management. Each day they list and prioritize their goals, concentrating on the most important things first, but always one thing at a time.

CHAPTER 11
Hidden Meanings in Conversation

Whenever a President of the United States makes a speech, he invariably reads it, especially if it involves foreign affairs, because he knows that every word will be analyzed. That speech will be put under a microscope in countries all over the world, to determine what exactly the President meant to say. Every nuance and anecdote will be thoroughly torn apart and discussed, so that nothing can be hidden. Very often what's left out of his speeches is just as important as what's put in.

When you know that someone who's very skilled at analyzing conversations will be listening to you speak and analyzing your every word, it becomes very difficult for you not to give away the hidden meanings in your conversation. If you are aware, as you surely will be, of your own point of view and your own goals in a negotiation, you must also know that the person analyzing your conversation will quickly be aware of these aspects as well. This leads to two more considerations in any negotiation. Not only must you learn to be adept at deciphering the hidden meanings of the people with whom you are dealing, but you must learn to mask your own hidden meanings.

The necessity of learning to disguise your own hidden meanings should be immediately apparent. Nearly all of the negotiating gambits we discussed earlier are based on the assumption that you should have some secrets, such as how badly you need to make a deal, what the other offers have been, what your incentives are, etc. We have already discussed the fact that if the other side knew exactly how much you needed to reach an agreement, much of your bargaining power would be gone.

Another area you might need to disguise from the possible analysis of another negotiator is your "hidden agenda." As you know, an agenda is a list of the things you want to accomplish through your negotiating. But there may be things that you do not want revealed at the beginning of the business deal; rather, you want to use these points as the negotiation progresses.

When my daughter Julia came to me before her trip to Europe to ask first for spending money and then new luggage, both of those things were on her hidden agenda. She knew that if she asked for them up front, chances were excellent she wouldn't get them, so she timed her proposals to the moment when I had the least ability to argue. A hidden agenda is all of those things you'll bring up when the time is right during the negotiations. These are the points you save to propose until the point of least resistance.

If you don't work to disguise it, it's not difficult for another party who has studied the dynamics of hidden meanings within conversations to define your hidden agenda when you begin a negotiation. An expert at reading conversations can pick apart your every word until your goals are laid bare and he has you, for all practical purposes, at his mercy.

One defense commonly used by U.S. presidents against the hidden meanings that might be seen in their speeches involves the use of a press secretary. The President will often send the press secretary to make announcements without giving the press secretary as much information as he, the President, has. In this way, the President is able to protect himself.

I was recently involved in a negotiation that would have led to the merger of two very large companies. One of the problems that my company had—a skeleton in our closet, so to speak—was the knowledge that one of our major stockholders was in severe financial trouble and extremely eager to make the merger at any price. Of course, we didn't want the other company to learn this and went to great lengths to disguise this fact.

However, at one point in the negotiation the president of the other company said, "I am very concerned with the relationship between your company and your stockholder Mr. X. I feel that if we ran a credit check on him, we would find that he has serious financial problems."

The manner in which this statement was made puzzled me a great deal.

"Always listen for the hidden meaning in conversations."

The president hadn't said, "We have run a credit check on him," although that was easily well within his power to do, nor did he start off his statement with, "As you are aware, Mr. X within your organization has a terrible credit problem." He said, "If we were to run a credit check. . ."

His statement alerted me to the fact that the president of that company was in contact with someone from my organization who had passed some information to him.

Later in the conversation, the other president pulled me aside and said, "Roger, I know that you're an outside director of this corporation." This meant he was aware that while I did not work for that particular company, I did sit on the board of directors. He continued: "I understand that you recently spent an entire day at the corporation interviewing all the key employees. That is a very strange thing for an outside director to do. Why did you do that?"

My reasons had been very good. I had suspected that there were some serious conflicts within the ranks of the organization. The situation hadn't turned out as badly as I had feared, and that had eased my mind. But now, faced with his inquiry, I had some trouble answering.

I didn't know how to respond to his question until I remembered his earlier question and my suspicion that there was someone within my company who was feeding this man information. I realized from his question that he had already read even my confidential report of that day's activities, and so I responded in an attempt to distort the information he had already gained and that he could use to our disadvantage.

The lesson here is obvious: listen very, very closely to the words people use. If some comment strikes you as strange, jot it down quickly, word for word, and analyze it later. Why did the man say "my" instead of "our"? Or why did he say "files" instead of "file"? Why did he ask that question? How did he know about that? These are all questions you should be asking yourself all the time.

Very often people can say one thing and mean exactly the opposite. If someone starts out a conversation with the phrase, "In my humble opinion," you can tell that he probably means exactly the opposite. That person is not humble but probably quite egotistical. In fact, he apparently feels himself to be so great that he can profess to be humble.

When you ask for an opinion about someone and the person responds,

"He's a fine, church-going person," he could very well mean that going to church on Sunday is possibly that person's only attribute. Or if someone says to you, "We can just work out the details later," that usually means the other person realizes there is still quite a bit of negotiating left to do and that you're not as close to an agreement as he would like you to believe.

The classic in the study of hidden meanings is, of course, that simple admonition, "Don't worry." If your daughter calls you up at three o'clock in the morning and says, "Daddy, don't worry," what do you do? You start worrying!

There is a whole group of expressions that should alert you to the possibility of a hidden meaning close at hand. These phrases almost always precede an important part of a conversation. They are called throwaways — seemingly meaningless words which can point out important messages. They include "As you are aware," "Incidentally," "Before I forget," and "By the way."

Those four small words, "As you are aware," can be especially formidable. The negotiator could say to you, "As you are aware, I control fifty-one percent of the voting shares in your company," when there is a good chance that you were not aware of that at all. That statement, obviously a major point of discussion, was just dropped on you at the end of a seemingly meaningless sentence.

Often these statements precede an absolutely monumental announcement. The best example of this happened while President Truman was meeting with Winston Churchill and Stalin in Potsdam at the end of World War II. The war in Europe was over but the fighting was still heavy in the Japanese theater.

Truman had informed Churchill that the United States had developed the atomic bomb but had not yet informed Stalin. That night after dinner and a few rounds of vodka, Truman cornered the Russian leader and said, "Oh, by the way, Mr. Stalin, we have the atomic bomb."

Stalin responded calmly, "Yes, of course, we were aware of that." Of course he wasn't but he had to maintain his dignity in the face of that casual by-the-way. As you can see, even the most dramatic statements are made following an "incidentally"or a "before I forget," so prick up your ears when you hear these phrases and pay attention to what follows.

You should also be wary of legitimizers. These are the expressions such as "frankly," "honestly," and "to tell you the truth." These phrases are generally

211

used to legitimize a sentence that is not really true. When someone says to you, "Honestly, I don't think we could live with a proposal like that," what does that person mean by the word *honestly*? Has he been dishonest up until now? Or could it be he's just trying to make his argument a bit more convincing as he emphasizes that he is being strictly honest with you?

One of the most famous lines of all time is from *Gone With the Wind*; Rhett Butler informs Scarlett, "Frankly, my dear, I don't give a damn." Any student of speech could tell you that Rhett means exactly the opposite of what he is saying. He is using "frankly" as a legitimizer in his statement, trying to make Scarlett believe something that isn't true. In reality, Rhett did give a damn, and if anyone ever writes a sequel, we'll probably find Rhett and Scarlett back in each other's arms and living happily ever after.

Justifiers are words that lay the verbal foundation for the admission of failure. These are the expressions like "I'll try my best," "I'll see what I can do," and "I'll work to keep it under three hundred dollars." None of these expressions could ever be interpreted as a commitment, could they? These expressions are preparing you for the fact that the person saying them may fail, so unless you're willing to live with that possibility—and at the same time let that person live with it—you should challenge a justifier as soon as it's said.

Worse than a simple justifier, though, is the justifier transformed into the plural. Instead of saying "I'll do my best," the negotiator says "We'll do our best." Suddenly, he's hiding behind the group. No salesman worth his salt will accept the excuse "I'd like to think it over," but when the *I* changes to *we*, there is going to be real trouble. If someone has been using the singular all the way through the negotiations in his justifiers and suddenly the *I* becomes plural, the salesman had better realize he's in serious trouble and that if he wants to make a sale, he will have to return to the fray and do some quick selling.

Another language tool is the eraser. There are many of these but the most popular are undoubtedly "but" and "however." The important thing to notice about these words is their amazing ability to erase everything that has been said before. Someone can rattle on for ten minutes about how much he enjoys your product and how he certainly never considers buying any product but yours and then finish his ten minute discourse with a but or a however and completely erase everything he has just said. You know you'll

212

have to start over from scratch with your presentation because with an eraser, he has just removed all of your arguments.

The danger of the eraser is compounded when that phrase is preceded by a sentence such as "I'm just a country boy" or "I'm no student of the law" or "I never graduated from college." These are called deceptions. "I've never fully understood this theory, but. . ." enables the speaker to come up with almost any criticism he feels like. How about "I know it's none of my business, but. . ."? Hasn't that speaker just insinuated himself into a position where he can say almost anything? These phrases are often untrue, at the least, and they always live up to their name. They try to lead the listeners into a more relaxed atmosphere — declaring that the speaker is in some ways inferior and therefore not to expect too much from him. The speaker is lulling his listeners into expecting a weak, possibly stupid statement, in order to flummox them with a surprisingly astute observation. The danger of this cannot be overestimated.

President Lyndon Johnson was faced with this situation once. He was approached by a politician who began his proposal with, "Mr. President, I'm just a country boy. . ." Johnson exploded.

"For your information," he said, "I happen to be a country boy as well, and in this town, when someone says that to me, I have the urge to keep my hand on my wallet."

If someone begins his rebuttal with "Roger, I'm no student of the law, but. . ." I know immediately that he may not have completed formal legal studies, but I have no doubt he'll know exactly what he's talking about.

I have already mentioned preparers in an earlier chapter. These phrases are extremely important to salespeople and loan officers. They include the ever popular "I don't mean to be personal. . ." The speaker may really not want to be personal but in saying that, hasn't he just given himself permission to ask you about anything from your birthdate to your sex life? When someone tells you he doesn't want to get personal, be assured he's about to get very personal.

When a salesman says, "I don't want to intrude," what is he about to do? You know as well as I do he's getting ready to intrude. He's just going out of his way to prepare you for it.

Another way to prepare people for potentially difficult questions is to exaggerate the situation. Let's say that the fat little man at the bank wants

213

to ask you what your income was last year as you are filling out your credit application. He says to you, "This is very embarrassing for me, but. . ." In the three seconds from the time he begins preparing until he finally spits out the question, all sorts of things run through your mind. You are wondering just how embarrassing this is going to be, and when you find out that the only thing he wants to know is your income, the question is much easier to swallow.

Someone might approach you and say, "I need a big, big favor." You guess he's about to ask you for a thousand dollars, or at the very least, five hundred, so when he asks you for seventy-five, the big favor seems much smaller than you anticipated and you're much more likely to agree. But you are still paying seventy-five dollars, so if you have your doubts, be careful about the exaggeration ploy.

In the negotiating process you will frequently encounter "trial balloons." These are the sort of statements that start off with "I haven't really given this a whole lot of thought yet, but what do you think about. . ." or "Just off the top of my head, suppose that we. . ." In this case you can be fairly sure that the speaker has already made up his mind to try something but he's not sure if you're going to go along with his idea, so he's sending up a small trial balloon.

This trial balloon can tell you two things. First of all, the speaker will support whatever he is suggesting, no matter how off the top of his head he claims it to be or however little thought he claims to have put into it. In effect, he has narrowed his negotiating range by proposing a solution he will be happy with.

Secondly, the trial balloon tells you the speaker has doubts about the possibilities of his suggestion—he's not sure if it really is such a good idea. The speaker definitely has his doubts about the idea's appeal to you. This allows you to judge the proposal, and if it's not exactly what you want, you are in a position to try and push a little harder for what you want.

Another important aspect of conversation often overlooked can be an indispensable aid in your search for hidden meanings: the tendency everyone has to be oriented to one particular sense. We all interpret everything we experience through our different senses: sight, hearing, smell, taste, and touch. At the same time, notice that each of us has a particular strength in the area of one particular sense. Taste is the most unusual sense for a

214

person to be oriented toward, while the most popular senses are sight, hearing, and touch.

You can define the sense of orientation of a particular person by listening carefully to the type of language he uses. Let's suppose, for example, that three people attend the symphony together: a painter, a poet, and a pianist. If you look at the professions of each, you would probably guess that the painter was oriented to the sense of sight and that the things that he sees will be much more important to him than what he hears or feels; the poet will be oriented to his feelings, that those things that touch him will have much more impact on him than what he sees or hears; the pianist, you would guess, has a greater affinity for sound than his companions, and to him, the world he can hear is the most important. As we can see, each of the three friends will leave that concert with a different impression of what occurred.

Although the orientations of the people with whom you will be dealing will not always be that easily defined, those orientations still exist and they can be very important to you as you plan your strategy.

As I said, a person will reveal his sense orientation through his speech. For example, a person whose orientation is sight, such as the painter, will say such things as, "Yes, I agree, but will the rest of my company *see* things my way?" He might say: "That *looks* very good to me," or "I *see* what you mean."

On the other hand, the pianist, who is oriented to the sense of hearing, would be more likely to say, "That *sounds* good to me," or "I *hear* your point."

Finally the person primarily influenced by the sense of touch and feeling will be the most likely to respond, "I *feel* very good about this," and "I think I can get him to *warm* up to that suggestion."

It is much easier to make the people with whom you're negotiating feel more comfortable if you communicate with them through the sense toward which they're oriented. For example, a visually oriented person will be more comfortable dealing with pictures than with sounds or feelings; he'll describe his opinions in visual terms and will find it much easier to listen to a person who talks to him in visual terms.

The visually oriented person is prone to say things like, "Let me give you the whole *picture* before you make a decision, or "I want to bring that concept more into *focus* for you. I understand that you think you understand it, but let me emphasize that things are not always the way they *appear*," or

215

"I hate to make you go over that again, but things are still a little *hazy* for me," and finally, "I can *see* what you mean now—the whole thing has become much *clearer* for me." Words like picture, hazy, focus, appear, see, and clear are words visually oriented people feel comfortable using and hearing. They all describe experiences in terms of sight, and for a visually oriented person, those are the easiest terms to understand.

For the person oriented toward his sense of hearing, expressions that concentrate on auditory experience are the most comfortable. He will say things such as "It *sounds* to me as if the deal is going to fall through," "We shouldn't be surprised—his actions *told* us how he felt," "He was coming through *loud* and *clear*," or "Is there really any reason why I should have to *amplify* what I'm saying here?" For the person who oriented toward sound, experiences will *tell* him things, aspects of the deal *sound* good, he can *hear* problems, he tries to *tune in* his listeners. The auditory person is the most comfortable using words like sound, amplify, turn up, loud, and hear.

The person who deals primarily with his feelings, what I call a kinesthetically oriented person, will express himself in a tactile way. "I wasn't *comfortable* with the environment in the meeting," "It was very difficult for me to get a *handle* on what they were talking about," "Perhaps, if you went over that point again, I could get a *grasp* on what you are saying," "I'm *anxious* about the bottom line on that project," or "Regardless of what you say, I don't think I'll ever *feel* good about that" are all statements most likely to be voiced by a kinesthetically oriented person. He is most comfortable using words that describe his feelings, both physical and mental, words such as happy, grasp, environment, handle, feel, and warm.

An understanding of the sensual orientation of the people with whom you're dealing can give you quite a few advantages during a negotiation. I have already mentioned that you can help everyone to feel more comfortable with you if you express your comments in terms that his senses can appreciate. This applies to your speech, but also to the manner in which you present your entire proposal.

For instance, if you are dealing one on one with a person you know is visually oriented, it would be a good idea to incorporate into your presentation a visual manual or a chalkboard drawing so he can *see* what you're talking about and feel more comfortable with it.

However, a visual presentation will have little or no effect on someone who is not primarily sight-oriented. A person whose personality emphasizes sound will not feel comfortable with a chart; in fact, he may actually feel turned off by it. Inside he might be thinking, You don't have to paint a picture for me—I heard you the first time. The person oriented toward the sense of hearing will want proposals expressed in auditory terms, just as the kinesthetically oriented person will most enjoy presentations that speak to his sense of touch and his feelings.

Be sure you mirror the conversation of others. If someone who is hearing-oriented says to you, "That sounds good to me," under no circumstances should you say, "Yeah, that looks very good to me too." Among people who study this sort of sense orientation, this is called a crossed response. You want to respond in the same terms as the person with whom you're speaking. He will appreciate that and be able to sense your position more easily.

Another thing to be aware of as we look into the hidden meaning of conversation is the speed of conversation. It's very important that you learn to pace a person in terms of the speed of his dialogue. If you listen to someone who comes from New York, you'll notice he probably tends to speak incredibly quickly, with a very clipped delivery. He'll talk and talk and talk at an exceedingly rapid rate, and when faced with a person who comes from Tennessee or Mississippi—with the slow Southern drawl—the conversation can be very frustrating for both parties involved.

Therefore, as you get better at negotiating you should work to adapt your speaking rate to that of the person with whom you're dealing. If he's talking with a Southern drawl, you don't need to copy the drawl, but do slow your words down a bit so that he doesn't feel rushed. If you're speaking with a quick-speaking Easterner, speed up your voice so he won't feel he's leaving you behind.

As you learn to pace your speech in order to adapt to different people, you should also try to adapt to the stances of other people. If someone slouches when he talks to you, it's very uncomfortable for him to deal with you if you're standing straight and erect. If he is acting very casually and you're acting very properly, he'll feel uncomfortable talking to you. He may not realize what it is that's bothering him but he will realize that the two of you are not truly communicating.

Watch carefully how the other person is seated. Does he cross his legs? Does his back touch the back of the chair, or is he sitting straight up? Does he lean his head back? Although I generally stress that sitting up and holding your head erect will give others the impression that you are a vigorous, energetic person, if you notice that the person with whom you're speaking is sitting in his chair in a very relaxed way, arms behind his head, chin up, then you might want to adjust your own position a bit. Try to look more relaxed yourself. On the other hand, if he's sitting straight up in his chair, leaning into his desk, and looking very powerful, then you should also sit more formally and present as much power as possible.

I'm not suggesting you take this to extremes. It doesn't take long for an intelligent person to notice that when he folds his arms across his chest, you do too. Or that whenever he sticks his legs out, so do you. If the person with whom you're negotiating notices that you're pacing his stance, he will probably conclude that you have just come from a seminar on body language or negotiating techniques and that might irritate him rather than helping your case. You want to be casual enough in your pacing without being obvious or obnoxious.

This technique of matching the stances of the people with whom you're dealing can be a very powerful negotiating tool. It definitely gives you more strength in communicating with people — as they see you mirroring the way they themselves feel, they think you must naturally understand their position in the negotiations, and so they're more likely to listen to what you have to say.

One more area that could be very helpful to you but has only recently been investigated, is the study of eye movement. Only within the last three years have scientists uncovered this fascinating branch of human communications. It's been discovered that a person's eye movement is directly related to what he's thinking.

For example, suppose you're talking with a good friend and you ask him a question. As he answers, you notice that his eyes wander so that it looks as if he's staring at the ceiling to the left. When you notice eyes moving to the top left, you may recognize that as a signal that your friend is creating a picture for himself in his mind. He is imagining not what is, but what could be. If your friend's eyes wander to the top right, he is remembering a picture. If the eyes move to the lower left, your friend is sensing feelings, remembering the sensations of experiences. If the eyes move to the lower right, your friend is talking internally. If you notice that the eyes move repeatedly from right to left, you may deduce that your friend is hearing words.

Remember as you try to use this to decipher what's going on inside your friend's mind, that as I say upper left or lower right, I mean as *you* see it. Actually, your friend is looking toward his right when you think he's looking left—so keep in mind that I am talking about what it looks like from your point of view.

If you keep this technique in mind and work on using it, you'll be surprised at how much it can tell you about what your companions are thinking. You'll better understand what others are saying to you. For example, if you ask a person about his business and you notice his eyes moving to the top left, you know that he's creating a picture and that what you are about to hear is largely imagination, not the truth.

In order to help you develop the ability to use this, here are five questions to help you practice. As you ask these questions, watch the eyes of your listener. *Do not* tell him why you want to ask him these because then he wouldn't be responding normally:

1. What color was the first car you remember your parents owning? (This should cause your listener to remember a picture, and so his eyes should move to the top right.)

2. What color is your dream house? (Here your listener will have to create a picture, so in all probability, his eyes will move to the top left.)

3. How would you describe the environment in your home as a child? (You have asked your listener to remember sensations, experiences, and so his eyes will probably move to the lower left.)

4. What is the best piece of advice you have ever been given? (Your listener would have to remember words, and so his eyes would move to the lower right.)

5. What is the sixth word of the Pledge of Allegiance? (The eyes would most likely move back and forth from right to left because your listener is hearing words.)

At first this technique may seem very difficult to you; it may seem like a lot of work for very little reward. But I strongly believe it can help you

CREATING
PICTURES

REMEMBERING
PICTURES

HEARING
WORDS

HEARING
WORDS

SENSING
FEELINGS

TALKING
INTERNALLY

sense what the people around you are thinking. If you will work with this technique and practice it, I assure you that you'll be able to understand many more of the hidden meanings in another person's conversation.

There is no question that if everyone were truthful about everything, there would be no need of tactics such as the ones I've described in this chapter. But since people do tend to try and hide things from others, it's essential that you learn to discern what is being hidden from you. If you can learn to sense even a minor deception, learn to feel when someone is comfortable around you and talking openly with you, your negotiations will be easier and much more enjoyable and profitable.

SUCCESS COMMENTARY

Keeping Your Uniqueness Alive

When visiting Rome a few years ago I was particularly over-whelmed by a statue of Michelangelo's in St. Peter's Cathedral – the Pieta, which depicts the dead body of Christ laying in his mother's arms. To see the original is a breathtaking experience – until I saw that statue I didn't fully understood a mother's love for her son.

There's a magic that exists in the original work of art that can never be duplicated. The people at Forest Lawn Cemetary once went to incredible lengths to duplicate the Pieta. They went to exactly the same marble quarry outside of Florence where Michelangelo worked as a young man and, having found a duplicate block of marble, used a new process to scientifically reproduce the original statue. Nobody can say that there is a centimeter dif-ference between the two – and yet there's no comparison. The original in Rome glows with the touch of the master's hand.

We live in a world of over four billion people and yet every one of us is unique and as incapable of duplication as that work of art. And yet we seem so intent on destroying our own uniqueness with an obsession to be like everyone else. The longshoreman who quits his job to write books of philosophy or the singer who decides he'd rather sail the Pacific Ocean shouldn't be news – a lack of conformity should be the norm of human behavior, the thing that separates us from the rest of creation.

That twentieth century master of creativity, Walt Disney, always bubbled over with new innovative ideas. In later life, when he headed giant corpora-tions, his executives tried to squeeze and pummel him into the corporate mold, without success. They were particularly bothered by his habit of publicly discussing his latest ideas before his corporations could implement them. "Our competition will steal the ideas," they would cry. "Don't worry," he'd reply. "I can think them up faster than they can steal them."

A great game to play for creative thinkers is: What would you do with your life if you only had six months to live, money was no object, and health no problem? Would you continue to work at your current job? Would you live in the same city? Would you spend your time with the same circle of friends? If the answer's no—why not reexamine your life so that you're doing what you *really* want to be doing. You're not getting any younger you know!

CHAPTER 12

How
Both Sides
Can Win

So far in this book I have tried to stress my conviction that in any negotiation the object is not to beat your opponent, but rather to creatively reach an agreement in which each negotiator can feel that he is the winner. At this point you may be wondering about this principle of win-win, and if this idea is really valid. For example, if you're selling a car and you want to get as much money as you can for it, how on earth can the other negotiator, the buyer, win in the negotiation as well, when what he wants to do is pay as little as possible for that same car?

I maintain that in every negotiation, no matter what the object of negotiation is, both sides *can* win. More than that, I maintain that both sides *should* win. We have talked about some of the standards of good negotiating, those benchmarks by which the value of a negotiation may be judged. These standards should not be any less lenient than those used by the silver craftsmen in old England as they hammered their mark into their wares. These standards can help you determine not only whether you won or lost, but how you played the game.

The first standard you should consider is whether everyone involved in the negotiation feels like a winner. You have probably not completed a good negotiation if the other party walks away from the table thinking, "Is he a great negotiator! I can't believe it, but he talked me out of everything!" Rather, a good negotiation has been completed when both parties can walk away from the deal feeling as though they accomplished something important.

The second benchmark is the feeling that both sides have each cared about the objectives of the other. If you felt that the other party was listening to you and at least taking into consideration your needs, and if the other party had the same feeling about you, then you as a negotiator probably succeeded in creating an atmosphere of communication in which a win-win settlement could be reached.

The third benchmark is the belief that should be held by each side that the other conducted negotiations fairly. A football team doesn't mind losing a game nearly so much if they know the other side was playing by the rules. A political candidate doesn't mind his loss so much if he believes his opponent has waged a fair and reasonable campaign. It's when there is foul play—a rule is broken or something sneaky is going on—that negotiations suffer from the feeling of betrayal one party will have toward the other. The attitude of both parties as they leave the negotiations should be: Well, they were tough and they fought hard, but they did listen to my point of view. I believe they were fair in the way that they conducted negotiations.

Benchmark number four: each negotiator should feel that he would enjoy dealing with the other at some time in the future. Like two chess players leaving a match, if the game was conducted fairly and well, each would want to play the other again. Not to outdo the other, or get revenge, but simply because the process of dealing together was enjoyable and challenging.

The fifth standard of judgment entails the belief held by each party that the other party is determined to keep the commitments made in the contract. Each side should have good reason to believe the other will uphold the conditions of the agreement. If either side feels that, given an opportunity, the other will back down from his promises, then that negotiation was not a win-win negotiation.

My definition, therefore, of a win-win negotiator is a person who can get what he wants out of a negotiation and still bring himself up to the standards established by those benchmarks. A losing negotiator is someone who has not filled the requirements of those benchmarks—no matter how many of his own objectives he gained in a negotiation.

There are five differences between a winning negotiator and a losing negotiator.

Narrowing to One Issue

The first difference is the tendency by losing negotiators to narrow the negotiations down to one issue. If a negotiator only thinks in terms of price during a business deal—when selling a car or a house, for instance—it is clear there will have to be winner and a loser in the negotiation. If we look at the Falkland Islands conflict and the kind of negotiation that took place, we can see that to narrow the problem to one issue—that of territory—would have to produce a loser as well as a winner. But as soon as we expand our vision to include the other issues involved in that conflict, for example, the prestige of the two nations and the prestige of the leaders of the two nations, as well as the economic and social impact of the conclusion, we realize that there was far more at stake than who occupied these barren islands full of sheep and shepherds.

Good negotiators learn to always look for the other issues—the smaller things behind that big stumbling block that are also important to the people involved. At one of my seminars a person came up to me and said, "I have been negotiating on a beautiful piece of property for almost a year now and it looks as if the negotiations are finally coming to a resolution. We've got the problem narrowed down to one issue—the price—and we're only fifty thousand dollars apart." I grimace whenever I hear something like that, because from that point on in the negotiation there would have to be a winner and a loser. If the negotiators had already resolved all of the issues except for price, there was almost no way both parties could win through a healthy give-and-take. Good negotiators don't do that. Good negotiators keep all of the issues on the table, and while they may resolve some of the smaller issues as they build momentum toward the big solution, as we discussed in Chapter Three with handling an impasse, *all* of those issues are renegotiable until a final agreement is reached.

Feeling Weak

The second difference between a winning and a losing negotiator is that losers always feel they have the weaker position as they enter the negotiation. Winners understand that the pressure to compromise is felt equally by both negotiating parties. Of course, it never looks that way. No matter where a negotiation is, the position you hold always looks weaker than your opponent's. It's the same principle we find with banks. As a person wanting a loan walks into all of that expensive architecture and impressive interior decoration and efficiency, he's tempted to think, Why should this magnificient institution ever want to loan *me* money? This thought arrives in spite of the fact that most banks spend millions of dollars a year in advertising and decorating in order to entice people to come in and apply for a loan.

A good negotiator approaches a loan officer at a bank with the idea that this loan officer probably just endured an hour of chewing out from the bank president because the bank has not been loaning enough money. A winner realizes it is very much in the loan officer's best interests to approve that loan, and so he enters the negotiations with more confidence and self-assurance.

If you believe you're in a position of strength, you will be a better win-win negotiator. For example, employees seem to always assume they're in a weak position whenever they apply for a raise or a promotion. They don't recognize what an employee's market it is right now in this country, and that in actual fact, if an employee is a good worker, his employer is probably desperate to keep him on the payroll. The employee sees only the limits of his options and does not usually consider the employer's options as well. The loss of a key employee could damage an entire organization. Finding, hiring, and training new personnel is a costly chore, and most people in business would rather avoid the hassle. Most, therefore, are willing to cooperate and compromise. A winning negotiator enters any situation with the attitude that his opponents will need to compromise just as much as he does. A winner will then conduct his business without the protective, even paranoid tendencies of the loser.

Jumping to a Conclusion

The third difference is the tendency that losing negotiators have to jump to conclusions about the needs of the other party. The most common conclusion seems to be that both parties are seeing the negotiation from the same point of view. It rarely occurs to the loser that it's possible for two intelligent, rational people to look at a problem and see it differently. It is easy to see that if I hold my arm toward you with my palm facing you, and you see my hand and describe it, you would probably give a completely different description than I would since I'm looking at the back of my hand. The descriptions would almost certainly be different, but is one more right than the other? Certainly not. The two descriptions are equally accurate, they have merely come from differing points of view.

My hand is something very simple, but most problems that require negotiation are not. If such a small thing as my hand leads to disagreement, how much bigger are the problems caused by real issues? Very rarely, however, do negotiators take the time to understand that neither position is absolutely right or wrong. Much of the conflict in the world today, I think, would be resolved if everyone would recognize that most of the time people are not right or wrong. They are merely seeing a problem from differing points of view.

We shouldn't compare the art of negotiation to a sort of verbal karate that forces one party to accept another point of view. A winning negotiator uses persuasion to lead the other party to see and possibly understand his view of things, and he is also willing and able to try and see the problem from the other side, weighing the needs of his opponent as well as his own.

I once chatted with the evangelist Billy Graham about this concept that there is really not an absolute right or wrong in the world, and he pointed out to me the existence of sheer evil. I must say that I agree with him. But while we must make exceptions in the theory for the Ayatollah Khomeinis, the Muammar al-Qadhafis, and the Adolf Hitlers of the world, a winning negotiator must understand that he is dealing mostly with people who are just as informed and intelligent as he is, and that the differences in position are merely differences in perception.

The process of a good negotiation, then, includes the winner's attitude that he must accurately ascertain and deal with the needs of the other party. Each point of view is unique, as a composite of all past experiences. It is a fatal assumption in negotiation to assume that everyone shares the same point of view. If a negotiator is a "cheap" person, extremely concerned with money, he may approach the bargaining table with the idea that money is equally important to everyone else involved. This is a patent fallacy. Many people are not concerned with money at all since they either have so much they don't care or they don't have enough to worry about. A losing negotiator will assume that his point of view is the universal one and will ignore the other needs of the parties involved. A salesman who thinks that all of his clients are concerned with speedy shipments—perhaps because of his past experiences with a few buyers—will make a mistake in the negotiations when he deals with a client mainly interested in guaranteeing a shipment at a much later date at current prices. The salesman may talk himself out of a deal because he didn't take the time to learn the needs of others. A winner never jumps to conclusions.

Lack of Information

The fourth point that could stop a negotiator from being a winner is the tendency to not get all the information he needs in order to position himself for a win-win negotiation. Losers often try to reach an agreement without knowing much about their opponents and the needs that they may not have mentioned at the table. I cannot emphasize enough that information is the key to success. Of course, to acquire the information a negotiator needs, the winner works to create a working environment free of suspicion and mistrust. He knows that if his opponent thinks he will use information to gain an advantage in the negotiation, there will be no way to get the information he needs.

It is certainly beneficial to establish a system of open and honest communication in any negotiation, where both sides may present their views and expect them to be respected. In this way, the information necessary for each side to help the other may be shared, and the path to a win-win negotiation is cleared.

The Opponent's Position

The fifth point that separates winners from losers is the unwillingness of a loser to understand or appreciate the position and the values of his opponent. A loser may work to gently persuade the other party to accept his own standpoint but he may have a great deal of trouble respecting the validity of the other party's case.

It is important to understand that every person acts only in his own self-interest and must therefore be motivated from that base. This is called "needs negotiating" by international negotiators. This philosophy stresses that people will act in order to meet their own needs, not necessarily to meet the needs of others. In order to reach a workable agreement the winning negotiator respects the needs and values of his opponent and works actively to satisfy those needs as well as his own.

Students in my home-study course (*Yes! Yes! Yes! Getting Them to Say Yes With Negotiating Tactics*, published by Plaza Productions, P.O. Box 3326, La Habra, CA, 90631; telephone 213-691-6306) are invited to call me whenever they're involved in a negotiation if they would like my ideas on arriving at a win-win solution for that particular negotiation. I get calls from all over the country and usually the caller is very excited about the project in which he's involved. The caller generally spends a great deal of time talking about the project, the potential for profit, and the opportunities for expansion. After some time, I usually have to lead the caller away from his topic and ask him about the *people* involved in the negotiation. You see, the key to a successful negotiation isn't the potential profit margin or the great tax benefits; the key to a successful negotiation is an understanding of the people involved and their needs.

For example, a student called me from Seattle. He was very excited about a piece of land he'd found that he felt was perfect for a shopping center development. He'd even gone so far as to line up a group of investors who agreed to finance the development. Then he ran into a critical problem. He found that the owner of the land was simply not interested in selling the property to him. Of course, this is one of the biggest stumbling blocks any negotiator can encounter.

In my seminars I ask a question of the audience. To the single members of the group I ask, "What is the opposite of love?"

230

Invariably the response is "Hate."

Then I ask the same question of the married members of the audience. "What is the opposite of love?"

Again invariably their answer is "Indifference." It seems that married people understand that love and hate can be very close. The true opposite of love is simply *apathy*, the absence of any kind of feeling at all. In negotiations, a negotiator is much better off if his opponent hates his proposal than if he is merely indifferent to it. If someone yells and screams when a proposal is made and says again and again how outrageous the whole thing is and how he will never in a million years accept it—you can work with that. Using the techniques explained in this book, you can counter almost any objection and eventually persuade a person to adopt a more receptive view. The person to beware of in a negotiation is the person who is apathetic because he really doesn't care a bit and there's no reason for him to change.

Such was the case with the owner of the land in Seattle. I asked the student to stop giving me the details of the land and the project and instead to describe the person with whom he was trying to deal.

"Well," he said, "the owner of the land is a very elderly gentleman, and he has a tremendous amount of money. He's very sick and knows he's going to die very soon anyway, and he just sees no reason why he should have to deal with me at all."

As you can see, I first took my student back to point number four, and got a little more information. Then I took him on to point number five, learning how to respect the other person's view. I basically asked him to walk around to the other side of the negotiating table and start thinking from the old man's point of view.

What might a person who is elderly, rich, and sick be interested in that would give him some motivation to begin a negotiation? It didn't take the student long to come up with an idea: perhaps he would like the shopping center to be named after him. The old man might be motivated to create a monument to himself—that would definitely be in his own interest. I readily agreed with this approach, and that idea eventually brought the negotiation to a resolution. As it turned out, this young student of mine didn't even need the help of investors because the owner of the land was willing to deed it over to the student's syndication for development in exchange for an agreement that stated that part of the proceeds would go into a trust fund for the old man's granddaughter. It was a win-win settlement for everyone.

In another instance a student of mine called me from Dallas. He was interested in acquiring a small business. While he felt that the business suited his needs and had great potential, he thought the sellers were being unrealistic in their asking price. He spoke on and on about the business and the possible profits, and again I had to turn him to the pivotal part of the negotiation—the people. "Tell me about the sellers," I said. "What information have you found about *them*?" He told me that they were a middle-aged couple with teenagers, which was basically all he knew about them. "What would they do with the money generated from the sale of the business?" I asked.

"Well, their immediate need is to get the four thousand dollars in tuition that it will take to get their daughter into a private college in the fall," he told me.

I admonished him to try and see the deal from the seller's point of view. "If this couple would need four thousand dollars in September, what would they need in January when the new semester started?"

"Four thousand dollars," he said.

"And the next September?"

"Four thousand dollars." By this time he was beginning to catch on. In fact, that couple would need four thousand dollars every September and every January for the next four years. Having looked at the problem from the point of view of this couple, the answer for a win-win solution occurred to him. Perhaps the sellers would be willing to trade the equity of this business for the assurance that their daughter would have sufficient money to go through college. That is the sort of solution eventually reached. This student got an excellent deal on the business by structuring the financing so that the sellers were paid four thousand dollars twice yearly for the next four years. It hadn't occurred to him that money was not the uppermost concern of the sellers, but rather, their daughter's educational security.

To assume that the needs of both parties are the same is a point we have already discussed. But it is a giant step from understanding that needs differ to appreciating what those needs are and creatively using those needs to reach a resolution. Above all, a winner realizes that money isn't everything. In any negotiation there are several ways to reach an amicable agreement which will please everyone involved.

The most important rule to remember as any negotiating is begun is to never jump to a conclusion. Never assume anything. And the worst assumption a negotiator can make is that a conflict exists between him and the opposing party. The belief that the needs of the two sides are so diametrically opposed that there must be a winner and a loser in a negotiation is rubbish. Good negotiators understand that a conflict of such proportions is a rarity and that with the skills and techniques outlined in this book, it is almost always possible (with the exception of the Hitlers and the Khomeinis) to reach an agreement where both parties feel like winners.

Spend some time with the ideas we have discussed. If you work to apply them in everyday situations, you'll acquire a surprising amount of control in any situation in which you're dealing with other people. Use these techniques to help you reach the level of success you desire for yourself. And remember that everything you need or want is currently owned or controlled by someone else; now you have the skills you'll need in order to deal with these people more effectively. It is up to you to use them ethically to reach an agreement that is to the advantage of everyone concerned: a win-win solution. You can have everything you want out of life. . . but you have to do more than ask!

Postscript

As I finish this book, I don't want to leave without telling you what a grand privilege I feel it has been to live in this country for almost twenty-five years. There is no place like the United States of America; it is the greatest country in the world! That may sound like a sweeping statement but I can prove it to you: *even the people that say they don't like it here won't leave!* (Even when I suggest that they should!)

I fell in love with this country in 1961, as I sailed into California under the Golden Gate Bridge. It was a beautiful place to come into this country, I must admit, with a perfect view of the richness and fulfillment America stands for. I wish every one of you could see this country through the eyes of a foreigner. You would see it so differently. . . . You would see the opportunities that exist here, opportunities you may have become blind to, having been so close to them for so many years.

As we sailed closer and San Francisco exploded into view in front of us, I could hardly believe my eyes. It was the first mainlaind American city I had seen and I was absolutely thrilled with it. I walked the streets of San Francisco for days, mesmerized by the gigantic skyscrapers, the flood of cars that descended upon the city every morning from the Bay Bridge, and by the many different peoples of San Francisco. I noticed the street cleaners as they swept and smoked their cigars, and the thought occurred to me that the streets of America must be paved with gold for anyone who comes here and wants to work. And after more than two decades of living and working here, I know that it's true—America is filled with the gold of opportunity for anyone who is willing to take the risk and make the effort.

Even after all these years, however, there are still a few things in this country that surprise and delight me. For example, it never ceases to amaze me that things actually *work* here, things that someone who had lived here all his life might take for granted—like the telephones. Telephones here work all the time, every minute of every day. You can walk up to any telephone in the country, punch in a number, and you will be able to talk to any one of two hundred and forty million people. And you can call through an operator, with a credit card, or with any of eight different long distance companies.

To most Americans that seems perfectly normal and that anything less would be a sign of corporate mismanagement in the offices of AT&T. But for anyone who has ever tried to find a working phone on the streets of Paris, or tried to put through a long distance call from Argentina, the American telephone system is phenomenal. It's practically incredible. The communications system here is so impressive, it just never occurs to many Americans that in other parts of the world, things like that don't always work.

Transportation works in this country too. I conduct over two hundred seminars a year, in conference halls in Fairbanks, Alaska, and the Virgin Islands. From San Diego to Boston, from Minneapolis to Phoenix, a plane is always waiting for me and the food on board is always hot. There is always a clean hotel room and a rental car available, no matter where I am. Nowhere else in the world can you travel and make the assumption that there will be a plane or an empty hotel or a store open when you need it. Things simply work in this country—the way they're supposed to.

The postal system works in this country. I know we all joke about the government-run post office, but we must admit that it *works*. Letters are delivered promptly—unopened. I can't ever recall having one of my letters lost or stolen.

The greatest example I have ever seen of what this country stands for and how it works has to be the 1984 Summer Olympic Games in Los Angeles. Ever since the Olympic Games were revived in 1896, countries around the world have taken on the responsibility of holding the games and making them a success. For the last few decades, however, the Olympics seemed to lose a great deal of their luster, getting progressively worse in their nationalism and their presentation as each nation claimed that the games could only be staged with government assistance on a tremendous scale and massive infusions of tax monies into the coffers of the games. But then in 1984 the United States of America said, "No. In this country, we have a better way of doing things, and it's called private enterprise." The people of America said they could stage the Olympic Games themselves, through private industry, without the need of taxpayer's money. What's more, *they did it!* I think it was probably the most magnificent Olympic Games ever—they did a splendid job. They even made a hundred and fifty million dollars in profit doing it, so you have to admit that all told, it *worked*.

As we work to improve our negotiating skills and perfect our abilities to get what we want out of life, let's not lose sight of the fact that ninety-five percent of the people in the world would trade places with any one of us right now! And they wouldn't be concerned with any of the things we spend most of our time worrying about, like interest rates or the next president or the color of the carpeting in the office. The very idea of living like the average American, driving a car like the average American, eating the same food as the average American—all of that would be heaven for almost any person in any other part of the world, and he would jump at the chance to come here and be just like you at this very minute.

With all of these opportunities and advantages, then, we should each determine to live our lives as the adventures that they should be. We should learn to savor each and every grand moment of our existence. . .we should appreciate every second of the privilege of being an American.